ClearRevise®

OCR Cambridge Nationals
Enterprise and Marketing J837

Illustrated revision and practice

Published by
PG Online Limited
The Old Coach House
35 Main Road
Tolpuddle
Dorset
DT2 7EW
United Kingdom

sales@pgonline.co.uk
www.clearrevise.com
www.pgonline.co.uk
2022

PG ONLINE

PREFACE

Absolute clarity! That's the aim.

This is everything you need to ace the exam and beam with pride. Each topic is laid out in a beautifully illustrated format that is clear, approachable and as concise and simple as possible.

Each section of the specification is clearly indicated to help you cross-reference your revision. The checklist on the contents pages will help you keep track of what you have already worked through and what's left before the big day.

We have included worked exam-style questions with answers. There is also a set of exam-style questions at the end of each section for you to practise writing answers. You can check your answers against those given at the end of the book.

LEVELS OF LEARNING

Based on the degree to which you are able to truly understand a new topic, we recommend that you work in stages. Start by reading a short explanation of something, then try and recall what you've just read. This will have limited effect if you stop there but it aids the next stage. Question everything. Write down your own summary and then complete and mark a related exam-style question. Cover up the answers if necessary but learn from them once you've seen them. Lastly, teach someone else. Explain the topic in a way that they can understand. Have a go at the different practice questions – they offer an insight into how and where marks are awarded.

ACKNOWLEDGEMENTS

The questions in the ClearRevise textbook are the sole responsibility of the authors and have neither been provided nor approved by the examination board.

Every effort has been made to trace and acknowledge ownership of copyright. The publishers will be happy to make any future amendments with copyright owners that it has not been possible to contact. The publisher would like to thank the following companies and individuals who granted permission for the use of their images in this textbook.

Design and artwork: Jessica Webb / PG Online Ltd
Graphics / images: © Shutterstock
McDonald's, Monopoly Cup © NKM999 / Shutterstock
Crocs © Avelina / Shutterstock
Five Guys Exterior © Ima_ss / Shutterstock
Point of Sale Display © Gulpa / Shutterstock
Nescafé Jar © chrisdorney / Shutterstock
Heinz Fridge Pack © Ralf Liebhold / Shutterstock

First edition 2022   10 9 8 7 6 5 4 3 2
A catalogue entry for this book is available from the British Library
ISBN: 978-1-910523-48-3
Copyright © PG Online 2022

This product is made of material from well-managed FSC® certified forests and from recycled materials.

Printed by Bell & Bain Ltd, Glasgow, UK.

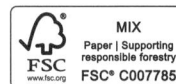

MIX
Paper | Supporting responsible forestry
FSC® C007785

THE SCIENCE OF REVISION

Illustrations and words

Research has shown that revising with words and pictures doubles the quality of responses by students.[1] This is known as 'dual-coding' because it provides two ways of fetching the information from our brain. The improvement in responses is particularly apparent in students when they are asked to apply their knowledge to different problems. Recall, application and judgement are all specifically and carefully assessed in public examination questions.

Retrieval of information

Retrieval practice encourages students to come up with answers to questions.[2] The closer the question is to one you might see in a real examination, the better. Also, the closer the environment in which a student revises is to the 'examination environment', the better. Students who had a test 2–7 days away did 30% better using retrieval practice than students who simply read, or repeatedly reread material. Students who were expected to teach the content to someone else after their revision period did better still.[3] What was found to be most interesting in other studies is that students using retrieval methods and testing for revision were also more resilient to the introduction of stress.[4]

Ebbinghaus' forgetting curve and spaced learning

Ebbinghaus' 140-year-old study examined the rate at which we forget things over time. The findings still hold true. However, the act of forgetting facts and techniques and relearning them is what cements them into the brain.[5] Spacing out revision is more effective than cramming – we know that, but students should also know that the space between revisiting material should vary depending on how far away the examination is. A cyclical approach is required. An examination 12 months away necessitates revisiting covered material about once a month. A test in 30 days should have topics revisited every 3 days – intervals of roughly a tenth of the time available.[6]

Summary

Students: the more tests and past questions you do, in an environment as close to examination conditions as possible, the better you are likely to perform on the day. If you prefer to listen to music while you revise, tunes without lyrics will be far less detrimental to your memory and retention. Silence is most effective.[5] If you choose to study with friends, choose carefully – effort is contagious.[7]

1. Mayer, R. E., & Anderson, R. B. (1991). Animations need narrations: An experimental test of dual-coding hypothesis. *Journal of Education Psychology*, (83)4, 484–490.

2. Roediger III, H. L., & Karpicke, J.D. (2006). Test-enhanced learning: Taking memory tests improves long-term retention. *Psychological Science*, 17(3), 249–255.

3. Nestojko, J., Bui, D., Kornell, N. & Bjork, E. (2014). Expecting to teach enhances learning and organisation of knowledge in free recall of text passages. *Memory and Cognition*, 42(7), 1038–1048.

4. Smith, A. M., Floerke, V. A., & Thomas, A. K. (2016) Retrieval practice protects memory against acute stress. *Science*, 354(6315), 1046–1048.

5. Perham, N., & Currie, H. (2014). Does listening to preferred music improve comprehension performance? *Applied Cognitive Psychology*, 28(2), 279–284.

6. Cepeda, N. J., Vul, E., Rohrer, D., Wixted, J. T. & Pashler, H. (2008). Spacing effects in learning a temporal ridgeline of optimal retention. *Psychological Science*, 19(11), 1095–1102.

7. Busch, B. & Watson, E. (2019), *The Science of Learning*, 1st ed. Routledge.

CONTENTS

Unit R067   Enterprise and marketing concepts

Command verbs ....vi ☐

Topic Area 1   Characteristics, risk and reward for enterprise

Specification point ☑
1.1   Characteristics of successful entrepreneurs.. 2 ☐
1.2   Potential rewards for risk taking... 3 ☐
1.3   Potential drawbacks for risk taking .... 4 ☐
     Examination practice ....**5** ☐

Topic Area 2   Market research to target a specific customer

Specification point ☑
2.1   The purpose of market research.. 6 ☐
2.2   Primary market research methods .... 8 ☐
2.3   Secondary market research sources.. 10 ☐
2.4   Types of data .... 12 ☐
2.5   Types of market segmentation .... 13 ☐
2.6   The benefits of market segmentation to a business.................................... 14 ☐
     Examination practice ....**15** ☐

Topic Area 3   What makes a product financially viable

Specification point ☑
3.1   Cost of producing the product .... 16 ☐
3.2   Revenue generated by sales of the product... 18 ☐
3.3   Profit and loss .... 19 ☐
3.4   How to use the formula for break-even as an aid to decision making ...... 20 ☐
3.5   Importance of cash... 22 ☐
     Examination practice ....**23** ☐

Topic Area 4   Creating a marketing mix to support a product

Specification point   ☑

4.1   The marketing mix elements for a good or service 25   ☐
4.2   How the elements of the marketing mix work together 26   ☐
4.3   Types of advertising medium used to attract and retain customers 27   ☐
4.4   Sales promotion techniques used to attract and retain customers 30   ☐
4.5   Public relations 32   ☐
4.6   How to sell the good or service to the consumer 34   ☐
4.7   The product lifecycle 36   ☐
4.8   Extension strategies for products in the product lifecycle 37   ☐
4.9   Factors to consider when pricing a product to attract and retain customers 39   ☐
4.10 Types of pricing strategies 40   ☐
      Examination practice .... **42**   ☐

Topic Area 5   Factors to consider when starting up and running an enterprise

Specification point   ☑

5.1   Appropriate forms of ownership for business start-ups 45   ☐
5.1   Franchising 47   ☐
5.2   Sources of capital for business start-ups and expansion 48   ☐
5.3   Support for enterprise 50   ☐
      Examination practice .... **51**   ☐

      Scenario and contextual practice **52**
      Examination practice answers 54
      Levels based mark schemes for extended response questions 59
      Index 62
      Formulae 64
      Examination tips 65
      Examination practice **65**

MARK ALLOCATIONS

Green mark allocations[1] on answers to in-text questions throughout this guide help to indicate where marks are gained within the answers. A bracketed '1' e.g. [1] = one valid point worthy of a mark. There are often many more points to make than there are marks available so you have more opportunity to max out your answers than you may think.

Eight-mark questions require extended responses. These answers should be marked as a whole in accordance with the levels of response guidance on **page 59**.

COMMAND VERBS

Analyse	Separate or break down information into parts and identify their characteristics or elements. Explain the pros and cons of a topic or argument and make reasoned comments. Explain the impacts of actions using a logical chain of reasoning.
Annotate	Add information, for example, to a table diagram or graph until it is final. Add all the needed or appropriate parts.
Calculate	Get a numerical answer showing how it has been worked out.
Choose	Select an answer from options given.
Circle	Select an answer from options given.
Compare and contrast	Give an account of the similarities and differences between two or more items or situations.
Complete	Add all the needed or appropriate parts. Add information, for example, to a table diagram or graph until it is final.
Create	Produce a visual solution to a problem (for example: a mind map, flowchart or visualisation).
Describe	Give an account including all the relevant characteristics, qualities or events. Give a detailed account.
Discuss	Present, analyse and evaluate relevant points (for example: for/against an argument).
Draw	Produce a picture or diagram.
Evaluate	Make a reasoned qualitative judgement considering different factors and using available knowledge/experience.
Explain	Give reasons for and/or causes of. Use words or phrases such as 'because', 'therefore' or 'this means' in answers.
Fill in	Add all the needed or appropriate parts. Add information, for example, to a table, diagram or graph until it is final.
Identify	Select an answer from options given. Recognise, name or provide factors or features.
Justify	Give good reasons for offering an opinion or reaching a conclusions.
Label	Add information, for example, to a table, diagram or graph until it is final. Add all the necessary or appropriate parts.
Outline	Give a short account, summary or description.
State	Give factors or features. Give short, factual answers.

TOPICS FOR UNIT R067
Enterprise and marketing concepts

Information about Paper 1

Mandatory written exam: 1 hour 15 minutes
Externally assessed
48 guided learning hours
70 marks
All questions are mandatory
40% of the qualification grade
Calculators are permitted in this examination

Specification coverage

Characteristics, risk and reward for enterprise, market research to target a specific customer, what makes a product financially viable, creating a marketing mix to support a product, and the factors to consider when starting up and running an enterprise.

The content for this assessment will be drawn from Topic Areas 1 to 5 in the R067 specification.

Assessment overview

The paper is divided into two sections:

Section A: 10 multiple choice questions with 1 mark each

Section B: 60 marks

The paper will consist of calculations, multiple-choice, short and medium answer questions, extended-response analysis and evaluation questions.

CHARACTERISTICS OF SUCCESSFUL ENTREPRENEURS

Entrepreneurs require a broad range of skills and personal characteristics to build and run a business successfully.

At the pre-launch, start-up or early stages of growth, the entrepreneur may be the only person involved in the development of the business. Being multi-talented becomes a real advantage.

Characteristics

Creativity

Creativity will be involved in the **branding**, product photography or **artwork**, **marketing** and website design in order to make the right impact and develop a strong USP.

Innovation

Innovation is required to make existing products better than others, or to develop new ideas or ways of doing things. This includes the internal operation of the business, its products and services.

Risk-taking

Entrepreneurs need to be prepared to take **calculated risks** in order to do things differently and stand out from the competition. Playing safe is unlikely to make much of a splash.

Communication

Communication is crucial at all stages of the business, from **pitching** an initial business plan to investors, sending the right **messages** through branded artwork, ensuring smooth **teamwork** and in **marketing**.

Negotiation

Negotiation skills are particularly important in **discussions** with banks, material suppliers, with customers and in hiring employees.

Determination

Try, try again. There may be many hurdles to success. **Persevering** after **setbacks** may be what separates you from the competition.

Confidence

Doing things differently to others can cast doubt on operations. Having the confidence to know that your new idea, method or offer is right can make the difference between success or failure.

A press release needs to be written for the launch of a new product.

Explain how effective communication skills would be required. [2]

Need to explain the unique features of the product[1] in ways the audience will understand.[1]

Sir James Dyson famously took 15 years and 5127 attempts at the first bagless vacuum cleaner.

POTENTIAL REWARDS FOR RISK TAKING

Setting up a new business or introducing a new product involves taking risks. Entrepreneurs will calculate these against the potential reward.

Financial rewards

A new business may not make millions, but there is the opportunity that it could, and the profits would be there for the entrepreneur in return for the risks they take in putting their own time, ideas, reputation and personal investment at stake.

Independence

Owning and running a business offers greater flexibility to do what you want with the enterprise and to choose the actions and directions it takes. As an employee, the direction of the business and working hours may be well out of your control. Many businesses are started by former employees.

Self-satisfaction

Many entrepreneurs simply have a passion for business. It can be highly motivating to create and grow an enterprise, especially one that aligns with their own values. The prestige and opportunity to become experts in their field may also be an attractive source of pride and achievement.

Make a difference or change

One of the biggest success factors of business lies in making a positive difference to other people and to improve their lives. This also creates huge motivation and satisfaction for people involved in the business. Some businesses are started by people trying to change the way things are currently done. This may be to put right a wrong, to find more environmental ways of doing business or to better support others in their industry.

Which of the following is a reward an entrepreneur could receive for starting a business? [1]

A. Financial security
B. Flexibility with working hours and holidays
C. Making a difference to people
D. Personal relationship issues

D: Personal relationship issues.[1]

With multiple choice questions, look for the correct answer, but check it by ruling out others that cannot be correct. You may be able to deduce the right answer.

POTENTIAL DRAWBACKS FOR RISK TAKING

The success or failure of a business rests on the shoulders of the entrepreneurs.

Many more businesses fail than succeed so a new business usually means long hours of hard work, worry and sleepless nights. What's at stake is a huge responsibility to business owners, including the welfare of their families and employees.

Financial risks

Many business owners will need to take on increased personal **debt** in order to fund a start-up. This can involve mortgaging the house, putting the family home at risk if the business fails. If the business has unlimited liability (e.g. a sole trader or partnership), the owner(s) would be personally liable for all the debts of the enterprise.

After paying all employees and suppliers, the business may make no profit at all for many years. This could mean financial difficulty for owners relying on a quick return.

Personal relationships

The daily stress of business, even successful ones, can put significant strain on personal relationships. The business can often be seen to 'come first' before family and other friendship commitments. **Divorce** rates with entrepreneurs are high as a result, but if the partner of an entrepreneur can provide stability and understanding, it can be highly productive.

Health and well-being

The **stress** and worry involved in all aspects of business can put a strain on owners' health, even when a business is doing well. Stress can bring on many ailments or can lead to alcohol or substance abuse which only makes situations worse in the longer term.

Work-life balance

It is important to find the right balance between work and personal life, to reduce stress and improve well-being. Many entrepreneurs find it almost impossible to 'switch off' from the business in the evenings, at weekends or even when they take a holiday which makes any **downtime** less likely to be relaxing. There are countless stories of new entrepreneurs working 12-hour days, 7 days a week. This means less time for **relaxation**, for family or for friends.

Give **one** way in which owning a business may improve work-life balance and **one** way in which it may worsen it. [2]

Owning a business may provide the flexibility to take time off when it suits.[1] Business owners may take more time for holidays.[1]

Long working hours may be required which come at the cost of social events/seeing their family/children in the mornings or evenings.[1] Business owners may find it hard to relax/socialise if they can't switch off from business problems during their downtime.[1]

EXAMINATION PRACTICE

1. Which **one** of the following is an important personal characteristic for an entrepreneur?   [1]
   A. ☐ Age
   B. ☐ Confidence
   C. ☐ Health
   D. ☐ Wealth

2. Which **one** of the following factors is not a potential incentive for new business owners?   [1]
   A. ☐ Being their own boss
   B. ☐ Financial reward
   C. ☐ Freedom to run a business their way
   D. ☐ Improved personal relationships

3. Identify **three** areas of an entrepreneur's life that may suffer as a result of risk-taking.   [3]

4. Give **two** examples when negotiation skills may be used by an entrepreneur.   [2]

5. David is a successful serial entrepreneur. He has started a new online marketplace business selling craft items produced by local artists and sculptors who otherwise cannot reach a market for their produce. 10% of the profits are reinvested into local community art projects.
   (a) Give **one** likely motivation for David in starting the enterprise.   [1]
   (b) Explain how the new enterprise may impact David's work-life balance.   [2]

   David has employed an agency to build a website for the online craft store.
   (c) Explain **one** risk that David might face when setting up the website.   [2]

THE PURPOSE OF MARKET RESEARCH

Satisfying customer needs is the key to success. One of the key reasons for carrying out market research is to find out information about what customers want. It will also give a business an insight into the market itself and any potential competitors.

Entrepreneurs should carry out market research before they start their own product development. They can also continue their research throughout the development period to assess the response to ideas, prototypes and different design choices.

Purpose of market research

To reduce risk

Market research can help establish whether there will be sufficient **demand** for a product. Without finding out this information, a business may produce and sell a product that nobody wants.

To aid decision making

Gathering information on customers, **market trends** and competitors will allow a business to gain a better understanding as to what products to sell, how it should promote them, where it should sell them and at what price.

To understand the market

Market research will include finding out about the size of a **potential market** or opportunity in terms of value, customer numbers, the products or services available from competitors and how they are received by existing customers.

To inform product development

Early prototypes of a product may be trialled with select groups of customers to get their feedback. This may inform further development to perfect the product and ensure it best meets customer needs. This reduces the risk of developing a product that is rejected by the market.

To gain customers' views and understand their needs and wants

By carrying out market research, a business can ascertain exactly what the customer wants. This will apply to the **benefits** they require, the amount of **disposable income** they can afford to spend on a new product, the **quality** of materials demanded, **when**, and **where** the goods or services are most needed. A company can then tailor their product to best fulfil those wants or needs. A new product often needs to be of higher **quality**, deliver **faster** or more **convenient** service, offer wider **choice** or be of better **value** to succeed.

To understand how a good/service complements others on the market

Research will be used to assess all other similar products on the market. This will include a detailed analysis of the prices they charge, the functionality of each product, their quality and the proportion of the market they each have (the market share). Entrepreneurs will be looking to identify a gap in the market where a new product could sit, or where a new product can fulfil needs that others don't.

1. Explain **one** benefit to a business of meeting customer needs. [2]

2. Analyse **two** benefits to a business of identifying a gap in the market. [6]

1. *By satisfying the needs of customers, a business will make customers happy.[1] Therefore they may see an increase in sales from repeat purchases and by attracting new customers.[1] / As a result, this would help the business to survive and become successful.[1]*

2. *By identifying a gap in the market, a business will know that no other business is serving the needs of those customers.[1] Therefore, by producing a product that does meet these needs they are unlikely to face much competition.[1] This may lead to a large increase in sales and revenue for the business,[1] potentially increasing profit.[1]*

   Another benefit is that by being the only provider of a certain product, the business can charge a higher price.[1] This is because if customers want the product, they will have to buy it from that business.[1] This therefore leads to higher revenue made per sale[1], potentially increasing overall profits. [1]

PRIMARY MARKET RESEARCH METHODS

Primary market research is new information that is collected first-hand by the business. It includes carrying out a survey, asking people to fill out a questionnaire, holding focus groups and carrying out observations.

Advantages and disadvantages of primary research

Advantages

- ➕ The information collected will be up to date
- ➕ The questions can be tailored to ask specific questions relevant to the business
- ➕ It allows the business to have direct contact with existing and potential customers

Disadvantages

- ➖ It can be time consuming to collect
- ➖ The research is open to potential bias, depending on the sample used
- ➖ Often more expensive

Primary research methods

Market research methods may be carried out **physically** (in person), or they may be done **digitally**. Digital methods may include CCTV, the Internet or the mobile phone network.

Focus groups

Small groups of people can be brought together to discuss a brand, a product idea, topic or issue. They may also handle a prototype or test a new food product.

- ➕ Can gain deeper insight into opinions or ideas
- ➕ Group researcher can direct conversation and explain questions to gather more detail or information
- ➕ Data will be exclusive to the company undertaking the research
- ➕ Can read body language to gain additional visual clues and opinions
- ➖ Can be expensive and time consuming as it is often tricky to organise
- ➖ A limited number of respondents can take part with a small group
- ➖ Not all members of the group may contribute fairly or honestly

Questionnaires, surveys and interviews

Questionnaires are carefully designed to find out opinions on something. They can be conducted through **surveys** either **online**, **in person**, by **phone**, **mail** or **email**.

Interviews are usually conducted on a one-to-one basis and offer flexibility for the interviewer to adjust the questions to suit the replies.

- ➕ Online surveys can provide a lot of data
- ➕ Questionnaires are a relatively low-cost method of data collection
- ➕ Can gather responses from large numbers of people
- ➖ Interviews can be costly and time-consuming
- ➖ People may respond inaccurately
- ➖ Questionnaires may get ignored as junk or spam

Observations

Watching how **people** (consumers) behave in different environments or looking at **locations**.

➕ Can be used to find patterns in behaviour

➕ Gives a true picture of behavioural response rather than how people say they may respond

➖ Can be time-consuming and costly

➖ Cannot reveal the reasons for people's behaviour

Test marketing or pilots

A new product, service or marketing campaign is offered to a limited group, store or area in order to evaluate the consumer response. New flavours of a product may be **piloted** in select stores only to begin with.

➕ Success of a product can be judged before rolling it out nationally

➕ Can help with predictions for the scale of a national launch with relation to stock, distribution and promotional offers

➕ Can get some legitimate testimonials before the product launches

➖ Results of a pilot may not be representative of the whole population

➖ Competitors will become aware of the product before it is fully launched and could use that to their advantage

Consumer trials

Products or services are offered before the business has completed all of the branding and marketing in order to gauge public opinion. In return for trialling a product, **feedback** is often requested.

➕ May encourage early adopters of the product once launched

➕ Often able to gather honest feedback

➕ Feedback may result in immediate adaptations to the product

➖ Competitors may become prematurely aware of a new product before it is released publicly

➖ Giving away free products can be expensive

➖ Feedback and opinions can be difficult to analyse

Yev has developed an early prototype of a product and needs to get some primary feedback on the function of the device.

Explain which method of research would be most suitable. [2]

Focus group.[1] This can be used to get valuable insights into people's real thoughts and opinions, whilst they handle the physical prototype.[1]

SECONDARY MARKET RESEARCH SOURCES

Secondary market research (also known as **desk research**) involves gathering data that already exists as it has been collected by someone else.

Advantages and disadvantages of secondary research

Advantages

- ➕ It is usually cheaper than primary research
- ➕ It can be less time consuming because information is more easily found

Disadvantages

- ➖ The information gathered may not be specific or relevant to the business
- ➖ The information may be out of date

Secondary research methods

Internal data

Internal data is that collected by the business themselves. This may include sales, accounts and customer data.

- ➕ Trends can be identified to help decision making and forecasting
- ➕ Highly relevant to the business
- ➕ Quick and free to access
- ➖ Data could be out of date or erroneous
- ➖ May not be helpful for launching new products into new markets

Books, newspapers and trade magazines

Books offer useful information but may be out of date. **Newspapers** are very current and often have a business section. **Trade magazines** are specific to an industry and can contain very up to date and relevant information. Articles may be online or in print.

- ➕ Easy to access information
- ➕ Inexpensive source
- ➖ Information may be incorrect or biased
- ➖ May not be a perfect match for the business

Competitors' data

Many businesses are required to publish their financial accounts publicly online. These can give clues as to their health and structure. **Competitor websites** will also have information about prices, features and sometimes a development road map.

- ➕ Information is free and easily accessible
- ➕ Direct competitors' information will be very relevant
- ➖ Competitors are unlikely to publish anything that would be useful to other companies
- ➖ Data for large companies cannot be easily compared to sole traders for example

Mintel, Keynote and Which?

Market research companies collect vast amounts of data and provide reports and summaries to their customers.

- ➕ Precise and comprehensive data
- ➕ Regularly updated
- ➖ High cost to access the research findings
- ➖ Research is likely to be broader and less specific for the business

Government publications and statistics

The government regularly carry out extensive **surveys** and have **data** on a wide range of areas. This includes the national **census** data.

- ➕ Reliable data source with no bias
- ➕ Usually free
- ➕ Quick to access
- ➕ Can be very detailed
- ➕ Can specify exact data and format
- ➖ Can be out of date
- ➖ Charges may apply for access to specific data
- ➖ May not relate directly to your business

You have been asked to research a potential new business idea for seasonal lawn care involving weed killer and fertiliser treatments in your area.

Explain **two** appropriate secondary sources you could use to gather data. [4]

Trade magazines could be used[1] to find out the most effective / best value chemicals for lawn treatment.[1] Competitor's websites may provide examples of the types of chemical used[1] and material costs for those could be found on other websites.[1] Government statistics could be used to find out how many people in the area have gardens[1] to get an idea of the size of the market.[1]

⭐ 'The internet' can be used to conduct primary or secondary market research but would not be classed as a stand-alone research method or source in itself.

TYPES OF DATA

Qualitative data is based on people's feelings, judgements and opinions, and cannot be expressed in numerical form. **Quantitative data** is numerical and can therefore be more easily statistically analysed.

Market research will be more effective when a business uses a combination of both quantitative and qualitative data. Managers need to be able to explain the statistics and figures that have been collected. Qualitative data allows them to do this.

Qualitative analysis

Qualitative analysis is helpful for getting a feel for general opinion but is limited by the amount of information that can reasonably be collected and analysed.

Quantitative analysis

Quantitative analysis is most useful for statistical research, making direct comparisons and drawing conclusions from larger scale data collection. Statistics may, however, miss some of the key, real-world issues, and the raw data can be costly to analyse.

Internal or external analysis

Once data has been collected, it must be carefully analysed to extract useful information from it. This part of the research can often take longer than collecting the initial data. Businesses can choose to collate and analyse it all themselves internally, or they may employ a specialist external company to perform the analysis for them.

FitTracker is a new health and exercise app idea being researched by a small software company. They are analysing the needs of the market using a variety of questions including those that ask for a score of features out of ten and others that require written responses.

(a) Analyse **one** benefit of gathering quantitative data from research. [3]

(b) Discuss **two** drawbacks of gathering qualitative data from research. [4]

(a) *One benefit of quantitative data from research is it is easy/quick to analyse large amounts of data[1] which can be turned into graphs/useful statistics.[1] For example, scores out of ten for the app allows the company to quickly calculate an average[1] to see which features may be better than others and which may not be worth putting into the design.[1]*

There is less risk of bias[1] when analysing larger volumes of data as it contains the views of many more individuals[1] so the exercise app is more likely to meet the needs of the majority of users[1]

(b) *A drawback of gathering qualitative data from research is that it can be less structured than quantitative data.[1] It is more exploratory because it is gathering people's opinions with varying lengths of answers.[1] This is therefore harder to quantify to get a solid statistic.[1] It can, however, reveal customers' tastes or dislikes to help improve the app design.[1]*

Another drawback is that it can be much more time consuming to collect qualitative data,[1] such as the feedback given in the written answer questions. This can take time away from more effective forms of research / tasks[1] such as software development.

TYPES OF MARKET SEGMENTATION

Market segmentation involves grouping customers together based on shared characteristics, wants and needs. Once the target segment is identified, a business must decide what its needs are and where to place its product in the market.

Age

Customers can be grouped by how old they are. Different age groups have common interests. For example, children's toys will appeal to a younger **age** range.

Gender

Traditionally, goods or services were divided into markets based on male or female **genders** according to their interests and needs. For example, aftershave is typically worn by males whereas perfume is worn by females. Additional gender identities are also recognised which enterprises may target.

Occupation

People in similar **occupations** may have similar needs. Categories of **unskilled**, **skilled**, **administrative**, **managerial** and **professional** occupations may be defined in order to target a certain group with a product based on their job roles or the likely income associated with those roles. Ties and shirts, for example, may be targeted at professionals and those with office-based or administrative roles.

Income

Customers may be grouped based on how much money they earn. A business may need to charge less to a lower **income** group or they may target luxury goods such as watches and sports cars towards the higher earning groups.

Location

Customers are grouped together based on where they live. A business may choose to focus on selling to people in certain **areas**. For example, a local taxi service.

Lifestyle

Grouping customers based on their **hobbies** and **interests** or based on the way they live their lives (e.g. health conscious and active).

Failing to concentrate on the needs of specific groups can mean no-one feels fully satisfied.

Franco runs a popular upmarket Italian restaurant and takeaway service for handmade pizzas. Its pizzas are made using the finest organic ingredients and priced above those of other competitors locally.

Explain **two** ways that Franco could segment the market for the Italian restaurant. [4]

Franco's likely target market is based on nearby location[1] as people need to be able to receive a pizza while it is still hot.[1] Since the pizzas are handmade and more expensive, Franco should target wealthier customers[1] who can more easily afford the food.[1] Groups who lead busy lifestyles[1] may like the convenience of a delivery service, even for an additional cost, which could widen the delivery catchment / increase the size of the local market.[1]

THE BENEFITS OF MARKET SEGMENTATION TO A BUSINESS

Segmenting a market allows a business to focus on the precise needs of each group. This aids satisfaction, provides a greater competitive edge against those who don't segment their market and improves customer retention.

Segmentation provides multiple advantages that each impact the others to provide further benefit:

Ensures specific customer needs are matched and met

A **niche** or small group may have distinct needs which can be uniquely met with a product or service designed specifically with them in mind.

Potential for increased profits/profitability

The more that people feel their needs are met by a product or service, the more likely they are to buy it and recommend it to others. This benefits **sales**.

Enables targeted marketing

Marketing costs can be reduced by sending promotional material and emails to highly targeted groups only. These include people who are most likely to become customers. Knowing the distinct needs of a segment also helps to get the marketing messages right.

Increased customer retention

Customers who feel well supported with their needs are most likely to remain **loyal** and continue to purchase from a business. This builds a valuable base of repeat business.

Potential for an increase in market share

Increased satisfaction in a segment is likely to increase sales. Overall, this may contribute to a greater whole **market share** for a business, especially if they can repeat their successes in several different groups.

The VW group make small hatchbacks, family saloons, sports cars and SUVs under different brands including Skoda, VW, Audi, Porsche and Lamborghini. This provides something specifically for each target group and for each budget.

EXAMINATION PRACTICE

1. Which **one** of the following is not a purpose of researching competitors' products? [1]
   A. ☐ Determine their quality.
   B. ☐ Find out what customers want.
   C ☐ Find out what prices they charge.
   D. ☐ See what products they offer.

2. Data that largely contains opinions and perspectives is likely to be: [1]
   A. ☐ Primary data
   B. ☐ Qualitative data
   C. ☐ Quantitative data
   D. ☐ Secondary data

3. Which **one** of the following is a disadvantage of using government publications in your research? [1]
   A. ☐ Generic information which may not apply to your business
   B. ☐ Quick to access
   C. ☐ Unbiased
   D. ☐ Usually available without charge

4. (a) You have been asked to conduct some secondary research for a start-up pet grooming service.
   (i) Give **one** advantage of performing secondary market research over primary research. [1]
   (ii) Give **one** disadvantage of performing secondary market research over primary research. [1]

   (b) Explain **one** impact of making decisions within the grooming business based on unreliable market research data. [3]

   (c) Explain **one** appropriate method of obtaining customer opinions for your business. [2]

5. Explain **one** way in which using market segmentation can help a business. [2]

COST OF PRODUCING THE PRODUCT

Businesses operate by selling goods and services. In carrying out all of the operations of the enterprise, costs will also be incurred.

A business should minimise costs. **Costs** can affect the amount of **profit** an enterprise makes as these must be subtracted from the **revenue**. Lowering costs will give an enterprise a better chance of making profit. To lower costs, a business could find cheaper suppliers, negotiate discounts with existing ones, consider its staffing arrangements or streamline its operations.

Fixed and variable costs

Fixed costs

Fixed costs are those that do not change in line with changes in output. Examples of fixed costs include: **advertising costs**, **insurance**, **loan interest**, **rent**, **salaries** and **utilities** (electric, water and gas).

Calculations involving different time periods

Fixed costs often apply to a full year or a month. To calculate the proportional costs over **smaller time periods**, businesses divide these up. For example, an annual rent may be divided by 12 for the monthly rent, by 52 for weekly costs or by 253 for a cost per working day.

Variable costs

Variable costs are those that will change directly with changes in output. Examples of variable costs include: **raw materials** or **components**, **wages** and **packaging**.

The formula for total variable costs is:

Total variable costs =
Variable cost per unit × Number of units sold

Costs per unit can be calculated by dividing the total variable costs, total fixed costs or total combined costs by the number of units output. This is helpful to determine if the total cost per unit is far enough below the selling price to create a comfortable margin of profit to ensure the future of the business.

! Note

- Loan repayments are not a fixed cost – only the interest charged is a true cost.
- Items such as 'salaries' and 'utilities' can sometimes be classified as fixed or variable costs, depending on the scenario. For the purposes of this course they are classified as fixed costs. Conversely, 'wages' are classified as variable costs.

★ The definitions of fixed and variable costs must relate to change in output. It is not enough to say that fixed costs simply 'stay the same'.

Finley's

Total costs

Total costs are all the costs added together that a business incurs in making a good or providing a service.

Total costs = Fixed costs + Variable costs

You may be required to rearrange a formula to find a component, for instance, to calculate variable costs when the total costs and fixed costs are known.

1. Finley is a licenced trader selling fresh fish from a refrigerated van at a market stall.

   (a) Identify **one** fixed cost that Finley is likely to have incurred. [2]

   (b) Give **two** variable costs that Finley is likely to incur. [2]

   Finley spends £1330 per month on variable costs and spends £6600 on fixed costs over the year.

   (c) Calculate Finley's total costs per month. [2]

2. Josh operates a competing fish stall. Josh has total monthly costs of £2400. He spends £600 per month on fixed costs. Calculate his variable costs per month. [1]

   1. (a) One from: Van insurance,[1] trader's licence,[1] market stall.[1] Accept other valid costs.

      (b) Two from: Fuel,[1] ice,[1] fish (stock),[1] bags/packaging.[1] Accept other valid costs.

      (c) £6600 ÷ 12 months = £550 + £1330 = £1880 total costs.[2] One mark for correct workings.

   2. £2400 − £600 = £1800.

In the exam you will usually be given full marks for giving the correct answer, regardless as to whether you have shown any workings out or not. However, it is a good idea to show workings out. If you make a mistake with the final answer you may still pick up a mark for showing your calculations.

REVENUE GENERATED BY SALES OF THE PRODUCT

Businesses receive income from the goods and services that they sell. This is known as revenue.

Revenue can come from many sources. It can come from cash and credit sales of goods, renting or selling assets, offering a repair service, or receiving a commission on sales if operating for a third party. A business should maximise its revenue opportunities. To do this, it could develop new product lines, offer sales promotions, find new customers or, if a product is in high demand, raise selling prices.

Revenue

Revenue is the total amount of income generated by an enterprise from its activities.

Business revenue can be calculated using the formula:

Total revenue = Selling price per unit × Number of sales (sales volume).

Rearranging the formula to calculate selling price or sales volume

Imagine the formula above as a triangle. Cover the figure you are trying to find with your finger and read the calculation showing. E.g:

Revenue = Price × Volume *or*

Price = Revenue ÷ Volume *or*

Volume = Revenue ÷ Price

Lyle runs a car garage offering a tyre balancing service for £30.

Lyle makes an income of £1,200 per working week (Monday to Friday) on this service.

(a) Calculate the average revenue per day. [1]

(b) The garage closes for two weeks each Christmas.

Calculate the projected revenue over a 50-week year. [1]

(c) Calculate the number of tyre balances done per day. [1]

(a) 1200 ÷ 5 = £240 revenue per day.[1]

(b) 1200 × 50 = £60,000 revenue per year.[1]

(c) 240 ÷ 30 = 8 services per day.[1]

PROFIT AND LOSS

To be able to accurately calculate profit, a business will need to know its revenue and its total costs. If a business can calculate these then it can also carry out some analysis by looking at what profit it will make at different sales levels.

Profit

Profit is made when the revenue received exceeds the total costs. If a business has total costs that are greater than revenue, it is called a **loss**. Revenue and profit are not the same.

Profit/loss per unit = Revenue (selling price) per unit − Total costs per unit

To calculate profits for a given level of output, you can use the formula:

Profit = Total revenue − Total costs

Tim sells filled rolls from a sandwich van to customers working on an industrial park.

Tim's fixed costs are £280 per five-day week.

(a) Calculate the fixed costs per day. [1]

The variable cost of producing each roll is £1.80.

(b) (i) Calculate the profit or loss made from producing and selling 200 filled rolls at £3.50 each. [3]

(ii) Calculate the profit or loss if he sells only 30 rolls in a day. [3]

(a) *280 ÷ 5 = £56 per day in fixed costs*[1]

(b) (i) *Revenue = £3.50 × 200 = £700. Total variable costs = 1.80 × 200 = £360.*

Total costs = Fixed costs + Total variable costs = £56 + £360 = £416

Profit = Revenue − Total costs = £700 − £416 = £284.[2] *[Allow error carried forward from part (a)]*

(ii) *Revenue = £3.50 × 30 = £105. Total variable costs = 1.80 × 30 = £54.*

Total costs = Fixed costs + Total variable costs = £56 + £54 = £110

Profit = Revenue − Total costs = £105 − £110 = −£5 (loss).[2] *[Allow error carried forward from part (a)]*

HOW TO USE THE FORMULA FOR BREAK-EVEN AS AN AID TO DECISION MAKING

A firm will **break even** when it sells enough products to generate sufficient revenue to cover its total costs.

Calculating break-even

A business must know how much it needs to sell so that it can ensure that the operation is viable. A break-even analysis is used to aid a business in making decisions about what price to charge, how much to produce and to help in managing costs.

The break-even level of output is the number of products that a business needs to sell in order for revenue to equal total costs. It can be calculated using this formula:

Break-even = Fixed costs ÷ (Selling price − Variable cost per unit)

You will not be expected to recall the break-even quantity formula in an exam. It will be provided where required, but you may need to rearrange it to find a missing number.

Reanna runs a mobile dog grooming business. She has provided the following information:

- Average amount paid per customer − £25
- Fixed costs of running the business per year − £7,500
- Variable cost of materials used for each dog grooming session − £10

Calculate the number of dog grooming sessions per year that Reanna will have to do in order to break even. [2]

Break even = fixed costs ÷ (selling price − variable cost per unit)

£7,500 ÷ (£25 − £10)

= 500 dog grooming sessions per year[2].

How break-even is used by an entrepreneur

Break-even analysis is particularly useful for new start-up businesses as it will allow them to see if their business is viable. This is because they will know how many goods or services they need to sell to cover their costs. They can then decide whether that is an achievable amount.

Break-even is used for '**what-if**' analysis. A business can change the variables, such as the selling price and variable cost per unit, to see what impact that has on the level of break even. This will also tell the business what might happen to profit levels, so it can make important decisions related to price, production levels and costs.

Break-even charts

Break-even can also be shown diagrammatically with the use of a break-even chart. In this chart, a business will plot its costs and revenues at different output levels in order to find out the break-even level of output.

When constructing a break-even chart, revenue, total costs and fixed costs must each be plotted.

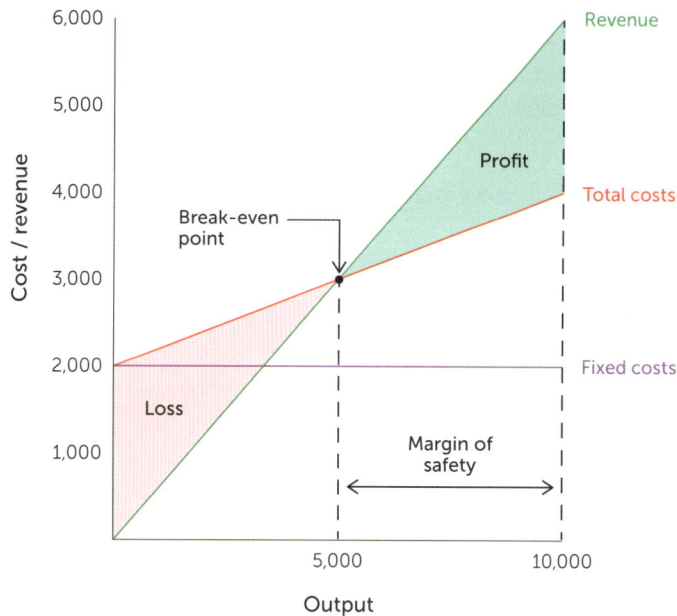

Revenue
Revenue is the **green** line. This shows how much income is coming into the business. It starts at 0 as no sales means no income. To calculate revenue, the enterprise must multiply the number sold by the sales price.

Total costs
The **red** line shows the total costs of the enterprise. This is calculated by adding together the **fixed costs** and the **variable costs**. A variable cost is one that changes with output. The total costs line starts at the fixed cost line. This is because an enterprise must still pay fixed costs even if it only sells one unit.

Fixed costs
The **purple** line shows the **fixed costs** for the business. As these do not change with output, they are a fixed horizontal line. Fixed costs must be paid regardless of number of products sold.

Break-even point
The **break-even point** on the graph is where the **red** and **green** lines intersect. This shows where the total costs and total revenue meet. This is the point at which the business neither makes a profit or a loss. In this example, 5 000 units need to be sold to break even.

> You will not be expected to draw a break-even graph from scratch, but you may be asked to interpret one or complete one that is already partially drawn.

THE IMPORTANCE OF CASH

Having enough cash is critical to a business. Many businesses fail because they do not have sufficient cash to pay all their bills.

The importance of cash to a business

A business uses **cash** to pay for all its day to day expenses. This includes paying its employees and paying for its supplies. Without workers, most businesses could not continue. Without supplies, the business could not produce goods or provide a service.

Difference between cash and profit

Cash is the amount of money that a business has available to pay for its day-to-day expenses. **Profit** is the difference between revenue and total costs. A profitable business can run out of cash. This is because a business records revenue as soon as a sale is made, but they may not receive actual payment immediately. In the interim period, large bills may become due.

Consequences of a lack of cash

If a business does not have enough cash to pay for its bills when they are due, it is said to be **insolvent**. This will lead to the failure of the business.

A profitable business has run out of cash. As a result, it may: [1]

A. Fail to break even

B. Go out of business

C. Increase its costs

D. Stop generating revenue

Answer B. Go out of business.[1]

EXAMINATION PRACTICE

1. Which **one** of the following would be classed as a fixed cost for a business? [1]
    A. ☐ Advertising
    B. ☐ Packaging
    C. ☐ Raw materials
    D. ☐ Wages

2. A variable cost can be defined as: [1]
    A. ☐ A cost that changes seasonally
    B. ☐ A cost that goes up and down
    C. ☐ A cost that never stays the same
    D. ☐ A cost that varies with the level of output

3. Roman runs a skate shop. In the period January to March, he generated £38,500 in revenue. His total costs for the period were £41,000.

    Which **one** of the following best describes Roman's financial situation for the period? [1]
    A. ☐ Break-even
    B. ☐ Cash poor
    C. ☐ Loss
    D. ☐ Profit

4. Jasmeen runs a small handmade chocolate business. She has provided the following information:

    Average selling price of a box of chocolates – £5.50
    Fixed costs of running the business – £12,500.00
    Variable cost for each box of chocolates – £2.00

    Calculate the total cost of producing 5,000 boxes of chocolates. [2]

5. Explain **one** reason why cash is important to a business. [2]

6. Caroline runs a riding school. Part of a break-even graph for Caroline's business is shown below.

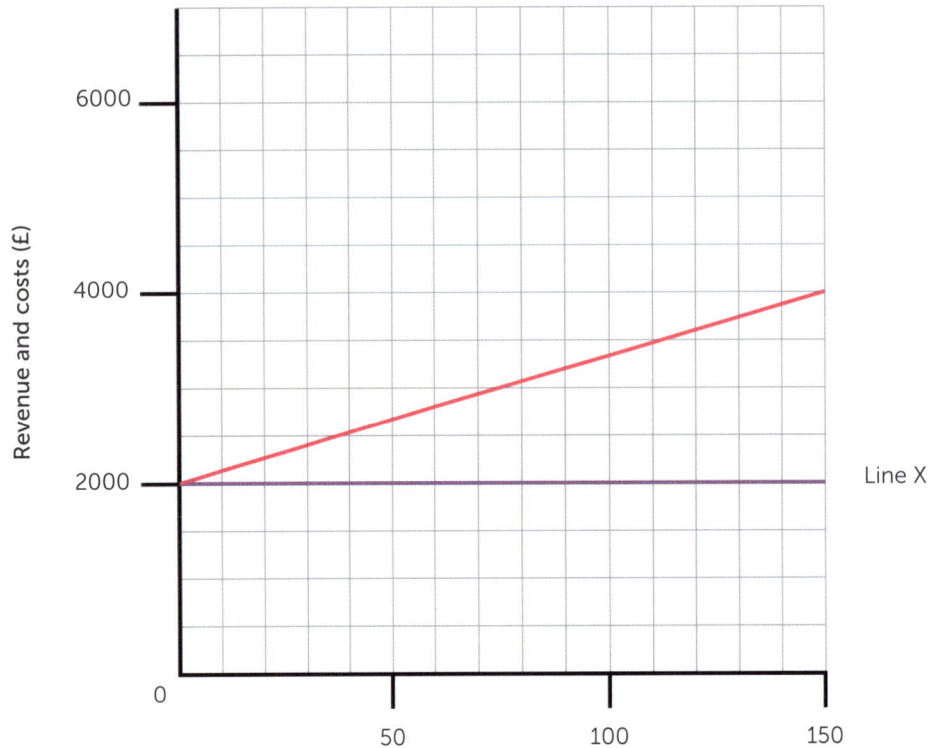

(a) State what is represented by **Line X**. [1]

Caroline generates a revenue of £40 per lesson.
(b) (i)   Complete the break-even chart by drawing in the line representing sales revenue. [1]
    (ii) Label the break-even point. [1]

(c) Calculate the monthly break-even point if each lesson costs her £15.
    Use the formula: Break-even = Fixed costs ÷ (Selling price − Variable cost per unit) [2]

Caroline thinks she can offer a reduced-price promotion to increase demand for lessons to 125 lessons per month.
(d) Calculate the minimum selling price she must charge in order to break even. [4]

7. Analyse **one** method a manufacturing business could use to reduce its break-even level of output. [3]

THE MARKETING MIX ELEMENTS FOR A GOOD OR SERVICE

The marketing mix is a combination of four factors – 'the four Ps' (**product, price, place** and **promotion**) which a business uses in order to persuade customers to buy their product. The mix will change over time and each element has an influence on the others.

Product

After conducting market research, a business will know the needs of their customers. The **product** (a **good** or **service**), through its features, design and function should meet those needs. The business needs to consider what will make its product different from others on the market. (See **page 36**.)

Price

A business must set a **price** (see **pages 39–40**) that enables it to make a profit. Therefore, it is important that an entrepreneur is aware of all the costs involved. A new start-up will often sell their products at a low price in order to attract people to purchase their products. A product that is of a superior quality may be priced highly compared to competitor products.

Place

A business must think about **distribution**. Distribution concerns how a product eventually gets to the customer from a producer. Within this element, businesses have to decide whether to sell directly to the customer, either by having a physical **location** or via the Internet (see **page 34**), or they could choose to use wholesalers and retailers.

Promotion

A business needs to promote itself to raise customer awareness of the products that are available. This helps to increase sales and build a brand image. There are many forms of **promotion** which include **advertising**, **special offers** and **public relations**. (See **pages 27–33**.)

HOW THE ELEMENTS OF THE MARKETING MIX WORK TOGETHER

Each element of the mix is dependent on the others to create harmony, but this needs regular tweaks and changes to maintain the right blend.

Influences on the elements of the marketing mix

Technology

New **technology** in the production process can help to lower a business' costs, therefore a lower **price** can be charged. Technology may also be used in a new way to create or sell a better **product**.

Market segments

A business will have to adopt a different promotional strategy depending on the **market segment** targeted. (See **pages 13–14**.) The ability of that segment to pay for the **products** must also be considered.

Competition

As **competition** increases it may mean that a more competitive **price** has to be charged unless the business is highly differentiated in terms of brand name and quality. A **product** may lose its **unique selling point** (**USP**) if a competitor arrives with a very similar offering in the same market **place**.

Product life cycle

The phase that the **product** is in will determine whether a higher or lower **price** can be charged. For instance, when the product is in the decline phase (see **page 36**), charging a lower price may encourage more customers to purchase it, or before then, a product may require an update, a refreshed packaging design or a new **promotional** campaign to be launched to extend the maturity phase.

Analyse **one** impact of changing customer needs on the marketing mix of a business. [3]

As customer trends change, a business may need to update the features of its product.[1] Therefore, there is a cost implication in designing and updating the product,[1] meaning that the business may have to increase the price.[1] Increasingly, customers are using social media sites.[1] As a result, businesses need to ensure that they are promoting themselves via this medium.[1] This will allow a business to stay current and help to maintain its brand image.[1]

TYPES OF ADVERTISING MEDIUM USED TO ATTRACT AND RETAIN CUSTOMERS

Some advertising mediums will be more appropriate than others when working with the 4Ps to devise a marketing strategy. Often, a combination of different mediums is used by enterprises to reach a wider audience.

A decision about which method to use often depends on the product being marketed and the target market. If the target market is more likely to engage with web-based technologies such as social media, then this may influence the decision to be made. Similarly, some groups are more likely to read newspapers, for example, so this may be a good strategy if an enterprise is targeting this segment.

Traditional (non-digital) methods

These can include methods such as **television** and **radio** advertising, **billboards**, **flyers**, **newspapers**, **magazines** and **catalogues**.

Digital methods

These can include **social media**, **pop up adverts**, **email**, **SMS**, **notifications from apps** and **influencer marketing**.

Non-digital medium

Leaflets

- ⊕ Cheap to produce and distribute by hand or by post.
- ⊕ Can include photos, QR codes, graphics and text-based information in a visually appealing design.
- ⊖ Often regarded as junk mail so can be ignored.
- ⊖ Short-term impact.

Radio

- ⊕ Affordable.
- ⊕ Wide reaching audience.
- ⊕ Can use jingles and specific sounds to catch attention.
- ⊕ Can time the adverts to appeal to listeners at certain times of day, e.g. parents on the school run.
- ⊖ No visual appeal.
- ⊖ Limited (often passive) attention from listeners.

Newspapers

- ⊕ Can include colour imagery and text to attract attention.
- ⊕ Lengthier information can be provided with an advert or sponsored article.
- ⊕ Targets specific readers, for example local newspapers are read in a known geographical area.
- ⊖ Cannot include animations, sound or video.
- ⊖ Limited lifespan of the advert since newspapers are typically printed daily or weekly.
- ⊖ Readership may be in decline.

Posters/billboards

- ⊕ Can reach a large passing audience.
- ⊕ Provides impact which can reflect well on a brand.
- ⊖ Not everyone notices posters and billboards.
- ⊖ Not so easy to target your specific segment.
- ⊖ Only a short-term solution.

Magazines

- ➕ Adverts are targeted at specific interest groups who buy the magazine.
- ➕ Magazines have a longer lifespan than newspapers as they often get read several times by different people.
- ➕ Can include lots of visual information in a glossy format.
- ➕ Content may also be published on the magazine's website to increase the audience.
- ➖ Content must be planned and submitted well in advance of publication.
- ➖ Cost can be high, even for a small section of a page.
- ➖ Reach may be limited.

Cinema

- ➕ Messages are delivered to a captive audience.
- ➕ Huge impact and attention with sound and motion.
- ➕ Can be selective with your audience depending on the film.
- ➖ Very expensive.
- ➖ Audience may not be interested in the adverts.

Digital medium

Websites

Websites combine digital graphics, audio and video with interactive features such as buttons and hyperlinks. This provides a wealth of well-presented and easily accessible information for customers. Most customers expect a business to have at least a website to find out more information about them and their products.

- ➕ Cheap to produce and publish.
- ➕ Useful for updating customers on new products or services.
- ➕ Can reach a global market.
- ➖ Still need to direct people to a website to see the adverts.
- ➖ Audience is limited to your own web traffic.
- ➖ Website maintenance can be time-consuming and expensive.

Online banner / pop-ups

- ➕ Catch attention and encourage click-through activity to a website.
- ➖ Pop-ups and adverts on search engine sites can be irritating or misleading.
- ➖ Ad blockers can prevent pop-ups from appearing in a user's browser.

Vlogs and blogs

- ➕ Can build a large audience and brand loyalty.
- ➕ Products can be promoted as part of the broadcasts and blogs.
- ➖ Influencers can command huge fees for promoting products on their channels.
- ➖ Commonly appeal to younger audiences so may not be as suitable for other segments.

Social media – Video, feedback and social networks

Social media marketing involves using different social media platforms to market an enterprise's goods or services. This could be in the form of a social network page or paid advertising. Posts could be in written form, short blogs or image orientated advertisements.

➕ Viral posts can quickly reach huge audiences.

➕ Positive third-party posts can be very powerful as independent, unbiased reviews.

➕ Third-party posts are free and take no time to plan and create.

➕ Some third-parties have huge followings and can promote a post far beyond the reach of a business.

➕ Reach can be global.

➕ Posts can be easily amended (if business generated), updated or reposted.

➕ Business generated posts can target specific groups with some social platforms.

➖ Business generated ads can be expensive and time-consuming to create.

➖ Risk of negative reviews or comments as a response.

➖ Negative comments or third-party posts can damage reputation.

➖ Third-party posts cannot be controlled or deleted – even if they exaggerate issues or contain incorrect information.

➖ Business generated messages may get lost in the billions of other posts online.

➖ Some legal age restrictions to use, e.g. Facebook has a minimum age of 13.

> Social media advertising can be business generated or third-party-generated. Business generated posts are those created by a business to attract attention to their products and activities. Third-party generated posts are generated by customers, rival companies and the general public. Depending on the source of the post, the reaction may be very different.

Podcasts

➕ Usually free.

➕ Can listen to them whilst cycling or doing other activities.

➖ Difficult to maintain a regular stream of valuable content to build an audience.

➖ May require a subscription to some podcast channels.

SMS texts

➕ Read by most recipients.

➕ Cheap and simple to set up.

➖ Limited in characters and cannot include sound or images.

➖ Irritating for customers. Often seen as junk and quickly deleted.

SALES PROMOTION TECHNIQUES USED TO ATTRACT AND RETAIN CUSTOMERS

Promotion helps to create awareness of a business and its products. Its purpose is to instil the desire in a customer to want to purchase the product or to be associated with a brand by building a strong brand image.

Promotional mix

Discounts

Discounting allows a business to attract customers based on limited time offers.

Benefits
- Can increase sales quickly.
- Can attract a lot of attention which drives customers to the high street or online store.

Limitations
- Reduces the margin of profit on discounted items.
- Can damage a brand's premium image if their products are discounted.
- Limited to short-term discount offers only.

Competitions

Competitions help to drive interaction between customers and businesses. They raise awareness and can be used to create a stir of excitement, especially if combined with an on- or offline advertising campaign.

Benefits
- Improves awareness of a product and market presence.
- Can help launch a new product or service.

Limitations
- Prizes need to be very attractive for people to bother entering.
- Competition prizes and promotion can be expensive if not outweighed by a successful campaign.

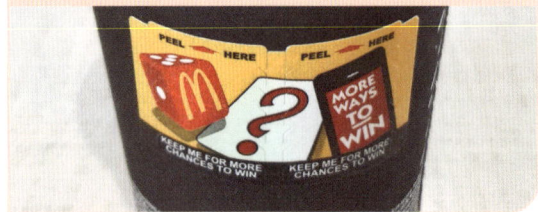

Buy one get one free (BOGOF)

Offers encourage greater sales, especially if they represent good value or something for free.

Benefits
- Encourages additional sales and promotes habitual use.
- May help the business to sell stock more quickly.

Limitations
- Reduces the margin of profit on selected items for the duration of the offer.
- May increase wastage, especially with unused food products.

Point of sale advertising

Point of sale (**POS**) advertising means positioning adverts or impulse purchase items beside a till (or online checkout pages) to encourage additional sales, especially while customers wait to pay in a queue.

Benefits

- Grabs attention from customers waiting in queues.
- Increases sales of selected items – clearance items are often positioned there.

Limitations

- Can be negatively associated with unnecessary purchases or junk food (e.g. chocolate and sweets).
- POS displays can be elaborate and expensive to produce.
- Limited by space surrounding the till area.

Sponsorship

Sponsorship is a method of raising awareness of a business' brand name in return for financial support of events or public spaces. For example, these events could be cultural, sporting or musical. Stadiums and even roundabouts are sponsored.

Benefits

- Can provide a lot of brand exposure.
- Particularly effective when targeting events for different market segments.

Limitations

- If the event being sponsored gets bad publicity, the business' image may suffer.
- It can be expensive.

Free gifts/product trials

Free gifts encourage purchases of a specific product, for example a magazine with a free lip gloss included. **Product trials** can range from a free square of cheese in a supermarket to a month's free access to an online service for example.

Benefits

- Can raise awareness (and sales) of a new product on the market with a free sample to try.
- Puts the business in a positive light – everyone loves a freebie!
- Increased numbers of customers sign up to a trial if they have nothing to lose.

Limitations

- Can be very expensive to package, post and give away products, especially internationally.
- Customers can get annoyed if they forget to cancel an online trial and end up being charged.

Loyalty schemes

Loyalty schemes encourage repeat purchases. They usually involve the accumulation of points (e.g. Nectar) or stamps (coffee shops with a 10th drink free stamp card).

Benefits

- Registered users generate valuable data on their buying behaviour for the business.
- Helps stop customers switching brands.

Limitations

- Difficult to end a scheme without upsetting loyal customers with unspent points.
- Administration of a scheme can be complex and expensive to upkeep.

PUBLIC RELATIONS

PR means public relations. PR usually focuses on maintaining a positive image for a business through press releases, building relationships with local communities or even engaging influencers.

Product placement

Company **products** are **strategically placed** where potential customers will see them and draw positive associations. This is common in big budget film and TV productions, but local business may gain exposure for their products in local theatre productions or at community events.

Benefits

- Can build positive product associations with large audiences.

Limitations

- Can be difficult for small businesses to find opportunities for product placement.
- Companies can command significant fees for product placement.
- Placement may not result in increased sales and may be negatively affected if the placement context appears false or unpopular.

Celebrity endorsement

Many businesses seek **endorsement** from **influential people** to help build their brand and the popularity of their products. Local, national or global celebrities, sports people or influencers may be paid to publicly wear, use or endorse a product, or they may be photographed with it. A local fashion designer, for example, may be fortunate enough to have their dress worn at a red-carpet event.

Benefits

- Hugely attention grabbing.
- Can create huge sales boosts and reach new markets.

Limitations

- Sales boosts may be short-lived unless ongoing endorsement contracts are agreed.
- Small businesses may find it difficult to afford paid-for endorsement by major celebrities.

Press/media releases

A **press release** is a short description or story of a product, event or incident that enables journalists to provide some accurate details in any publication. They are often used by businesses to raise awareness of a new product in a way that seems less like advertising as it is coming from a third party.

Benefits

• Can create mass media attention.

• Stories seem more credible even if they are largely written by the businesses themselves.

Limitations

• Some newspapers may ask for exclusivity on a story so you can't offer it to multiple agencies.

• No guarantee that the press release will be published or read.

• Usually only one opportunity to get a press release for a new product 'out there'.

Mears Smith is a garden centre on the outskirts of a town offering guided tours around their new show-garden with qualified salespeople.

A local newspaper has offered to write a story on their tour experience.

(a) Give **one** advantage of using public relations in this way. [1]

The company have donated their signature garden planters to the council for use as feature planting displays in the town centre.

(b) Explain why they may have offered free planters to the council. [2]

(a) *It is usually free.[1] The story will be impartial and likely to have stronger appeal.[1] The message can be distributed to a wide audience.[1]*

(b) *Product placement[1] enables large numbers of passers-by to see the planters which may encourage them to purchase them when they next visit the garden centre / to make a special trip.[1] This is likely to generate more revenue than the cost of the free pots/planters.[1]*

HOW TO SELL THE GOOD OR SERVICE TO THE CONSUMER

Place is a key component of the marketing mix. It considers a business' location and the method of distribution used. This determines how the product gets to the end consumer.

Traditionally, bricks and mortar **shops** and **face-to-face** selling have been central to any business, but as **broadband speeds** and new **smartphone technology** have improved, digital distribution of services and online sales have overtaken physical stores. Online stores provide **convenience** to customers and a quick, **affordable** and **accessible** route to market, especially for smaller traders.

> High street shop locations generally have a lot of potential customers walking past, especially at weekends. However, high shop rent and stiff competition from online retailers have meant many stores have closed.

Physical and digital channels

'**Bricks and clicks**' describes physical and online stores. Businesses do not need to choose between them. Many have a hybrid approach involving both approaches. Hybrid solutions offer more choice, greater flexibility and, potentially, a better service for customers. They can visit stores, see, feel and try goods on, then order them online later. Click and collect is another popular hybrid service. Data collected from online shoppers may also help improve services and product ranges in offline (physical) stores. Disadvantages include an increased cost of operating both online and offline channels, and difficulty keeping both operations streamlined with each other (stock numbers and the combined customer experience).

Whilst goods retailers find it difficult to operate without an online presence, the service sector, e.g. hairdressers and tattoo artists cannot offer online sales. They may, however, have a website.

An online presence with payment facilities is relatively quick and easy to set up. It is also relatively inexpensive compared to renting or buying a bricks and mortar outlet. The online-only option lowers costs for retailers, whilst maximising their target market and providing a potential for rapid growth.

1. Discuss **two** benefits of digital sales to a business.   [6]

One advantage is that an online seller can sell to a global market.[1] This is because they are selling goods on the Internet.[1] This may enable them to reach many more customers than if they used physical stores.[1] This could lead to increased sales and revenue.[1]

Another advantage is that they do not need expensive retail locations.[1] This may lead to lower fixed costs since they do not need to pay to open physical stores.[1] This would mean that total costs may be lower[1] which would allow them to sell their products for less.[1]

Digital sales methods

E-commerce

Any transaction that takes place online. Mobile and Internet payment and shopping facilities are commonly built into websites.

Website

Online stores or information offering 24/7 access to a global audience.

Social media

Effective advertising media to increase awareness and drive customers to a website.

Marketplace sites

Collections of goods and services, often sold on behalf of multiple independent sellers. Examples include Etsy, Not on the High Street and Amazon.

Online auction sites

Websites offering goods and services to the highest bidders, for example EBay.

Downloads

A way to deliver digital products or services to customers via the internet, for example on-demand films.

---

2. James receives emails throughout the day and night from foreign customers asking to buy subscriptions for his services.

Recommend an appropriate method of selling for James. Justify your answer.

Your response should include
- the advantages and disadvantages of **two** appropriate methods
- a conclusion. [8]

An online website with an e-commerce function[✓] *would allow customers access from anywhere in the world / at any time of day*[✓] *to make a purchase. Marketplace sites or online auction sites may be able to process a sale*[✓] *but then may not be able to provide access to the service.*[✓] *Face to face selling / a physical shop would not be suitable*[✓] *as customers are not local / would not be able to travel*[✓] *and James would find it difficult and expensive*[✓] *to keep a physical store open 24/7.*[✓]

In conclusion, a website with an e-commerce facility would be the most efficient and effective thing to implement[✓] *as it provides access to a global customer base and is not restricted by opening hours.*[✓] *This type of question will be marked using a Levels Based Marks Scheme. See page 59 for details.*

THE PRODUCT LIFE CYCLE

Businesses use the **product life cycle** to evaluate product life span. The product life cycle is a method that describes a product's stages from its introduction to the market until it is removed from the market. There are five stages: **development**, **introduction**, **growth**, **maturity**, and **decline**.

The phases of the product life cycle

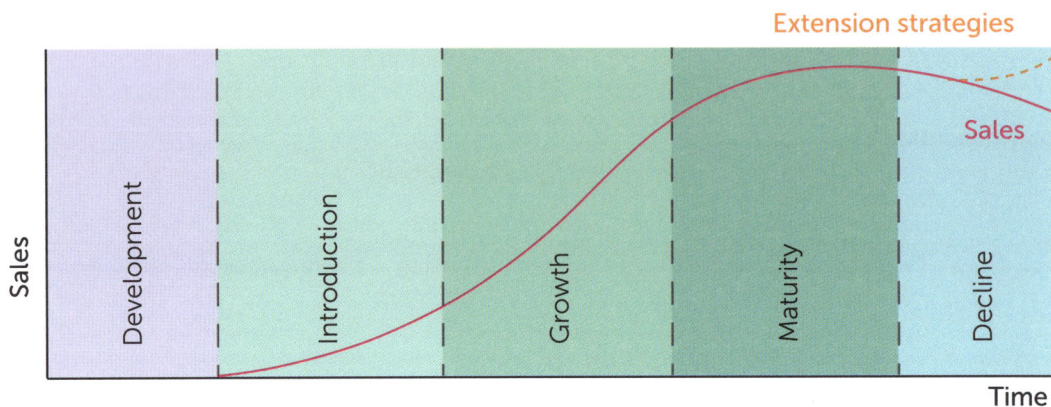

Development	Introduction	Growth	Maturity	Decline
Research and development is employed to come up with a marketable product. As this is pre-launch, no sales are made, but the business incurs lots of costs, so related cash-flow is negative.	The product is launched onto the market. Sales start to increase. Cash-flow is likely to remain negative as the business must heavily promote the product to develop awareness of it.	Sales will start to rise more rapidly after a successful launch as customers become more familiar with the product. As sales start to rise, cash-flow starts to become positive.	Sales levels and cash-flow are at their highest. However, growth in sales will start to slow down. The market may become saturated as more competitors enter the market.	Sales of the product decrease. This may be because the product is outdated. If this continues, the business may decide to withdraw the product.

Brenda sells burgers on a food truck. Brenda has noticed that the truck's new homemade vegan burger has become much more popular over the last few months.

Identify the likely position of the vegan burger on the product life cycle. [1]

Growth stage.[1]

! Note

Different products can be at different stages of this product life cycle at different times. Not all products reach the decline stage. Consider Coca-Cola. This product continues to be at the maturity stage despite being released over 100 years ago.

EXTENSION STRATEGIES FOR PRODUCTS IN THE PRODUCT LIFE CYCLE

Before a business' product enters the decline phase, a business can use an extension strategy to extend the maturity phase of the life cycle.

'Product' refers to both goods and services.

Extension strategies

Advertising

A change of strategy in advertising or promotional campaign can create an uplift in sales of a declining product. This may appeal to new people or remind past customers of its existence to an extent that they make a new purchase. Crocs shoes had a massive resurgence in 2022 thanks to collaborations with **celebrities** and the advertising that came with that.

➕ Serves as a useful reminder of a product's existence and benefits

➕ Can target a specific segment of the market to stimulate sales

➖ Needs to be ongoing in order to maintain effectiveness

➖ Can be expensive, especially with national campaigns

Adding value

(Improving the specification of an existing product.)

Companies may choose to **update a product** to improve its specification as it enters the decline phase of the life cycle. Imagine a version upgrade, a new range of colours, a longer lasting food or a more sustainable product edition. Nescafé launched a 'new improved flavour' in 2021 to extend the sales of their original instant coffee. Businesses may also bundle together additional extras with products, for example free accessories or an extended service contract.

➕ Improves desirability where a product meets the needs of more customers

➖ Product development can be costly

Price changes

Discounting or reducing price as a product declines in sales can increase the demand for it, especially where customers could not afford the initial price. This method is popular with companies using **price skimming** where brand image is not affected by cheaper prices. Novels are often launched at a premium price which then drops over time to keep sales volumes high.

➕ Customers may switch from other, more expensive, brands

➖ Reducing price means reducing profits

→

Exploration of new markets (geographic or target market)

Once a product reaches decline in one market, there may be another market that opens up. This could potentially start the life cycle again at the introduction or growth stages, increasing the life and revenue of the product. This may apply to different market segments within the same region, or it could be a new city, country or overseas market, for example. Restaurant chains typically maintain maturity and growth by opening new stores in new locations or countries.

- ⊕ Provides opportunity for new sales growth
- ⊕ Spreads the balance of decline and growth over multiple markets
- ⊖ Product needs to suit the new market and be accepted

New packaging

New packaging can refresh an existing product, giving it a newer and more appealing look. Heinz introduced the fridge pack which keeps beans fresher for longer once opened and offers portion control indicators down the side.

- ⊕ A new look can appeal to a new segment
- ⊕ May appear to be a newer or better product
- ⊕ New packaging may be cheaper or more environmentally friendly to produce
- ⊖ Customers aren't fooled so easily and may respond negatively
- ⊖ Regular customers may no longer recognise the product
- ⊖ Costs of design and production of new packaging may increase the price of the product

FACTORS TO CONSIDER WHEN PRICING A PRODUCT TO ATTRACT AND RETAIN CUSTOMERS

The **price** a business charges plays an important role in developing a successful marketing mix.

Retaining customers is never easy, and attracting them in the first place is even harder for businesses. Price can play a key role in the buying decision so should be carefully considered.

Income levels of target customers

Customers can only purchase what they can afford, so increasing price, decreases your market. Some customer groups are more sensitive to price than others. Those with young families, for example, will have lower **disposable incomes**.

Income levels will affect the potential value of a product to people. A business's pricing strategy needs to consider the likely value on their primary target market.

Price of competitor products

Customers will naturally compare like for like across brands so businesses should consider how their products will compete on price. For some markets, price will be a key buying factor.

Cost of production

The price of a product must be greater than the cost to develop the product in order to cover costs and make a **profit**. Whilst some businesses offer products at or below cost to try to increase market share by attracting new customers, this is not sustainable for very long.

Stage of the product life cycle

If a product has been identified as in decline, a decision could be made to reduce the price to increase sales again as an **extension strategy**.

Hamed has started a sole trader business selling plain sports clothing at a busy daily market.

Analyse which factor is most important to Hamed in deciding what prices to charge. [3]

Customers visiting a market are likely to have lower disposable incomes than those visiting established stores.[1] They may also be looking for a bargain/value.[1] As a result, Hamed will need to make his products affordable.[1]

Hamed will need to price his products similarly to other traders of similar goods (as he has a limited USP with plain sports clothing), and below those of stores who can offer guarantees and returns.[1] Consequently, this could lead to the business not selling enough products to breakeven.[1]

TYPES OF PRICING STRATEGIES

Price is the value that is placed on a good or service offered. When marketing a product, it is important to set the correct price.

Many factors affect price depending on the **product**, its quality, the method of **promotion** the enterprise wishes to use, the **place** it is being sold and what the competitors are charging. Based on these factors an enterprise can use various different pricing strategies. A pricing strategy is a way of setting a price so that the enterprise can achieve its marketing aims and objectives.

Price penetration

Price penetration sets a lower price when a product is introduced to the market which increases as the product becomes more established. This helps the good or service to enter the market and gather an existing customer base who hopefully remain loyal to the brand.

Advantages
- Helps establish a market share by getting more products out there
- Discourages competitors from entering the market

Disadvantages
- Results in a much lower profit per unit
- Customers may not want to buy anymore once prices increase
- Price may be associated with quality which may put off some buyers

Price skimming

Price skimming sets a high initial price, usually because the product might be highly desired or of superior quality to competing products. As the product or service ages, the price lowers to try to continually attract new customers. Games console manufacturers often use this strategy.

Advantages
- Helps to recover product research and development costs more quickly
- Where price is associated with quality, a higher price may actually help sales
- Lowering prices over time can help prolong the maturity stage of the product life cycle

Disadvantages
- High prices may naturally put off some buyers in favour of cheaper alternatives
- High prices may attract competitors who think they can offer the same for less

Competitive pricing

Competitive pricing means that enterprises set their prices based on those of their competitors. They often try to undercut them or to at least match their prices. Some deliberately charge more to create a perception of quality.

Advantages

- Can quickly increase market share and profit margins
- Low risk and involves little research

Disadvantages

- Need to be certain that your competitor's products are correctly priced before you follow their strategy
- May mean you miss out on longer term opportunities

Psychological pricing

Psychological pricing is used to create an illusion of value. For example, setting prices at £9.99 instead of £10.00 seems more attractive, which helps to encourage sales.

Advantages

- Encourages sales as prices are seen as being lower than they really are
- Can create a valuable reputation of low prices

Disadvantages

- Difficult to apply discount percentages to prices to the exact pence as rounding errors occur
- People are becoming wise to the strategy so it is less and less effective

---

Mankish has recently opened a Turkish barber in a busy city high street.

When he opened the new store in May, he offered cuts at a very low price for the summer before raising them to match other barbers in the area.

(a) State the name of the pricing strategy Mankish used for the opening summer. [1]

(b) Explain **one** disadvantage of using competitive pricing for Mankish. [2]

(a) Price penetration.[1]

(b) Mankish is less well established than the competition[1] and low initial prices may not cover the start up and running costs.[1] Competitive pricing assumes others have set the right price[1] but they may be in financial trouble and matching their errors may be a mistake.[1] / Competitive pricing only really works if your good or service has better features than the competition.[1]

EXAMINATION PRACTICE

1. Which **one** of the following is not part of the marketing mix? [1]

    A. ☐ Price.

    B. ☐ Place.

    C. ☐ Profit.

    D. ☐ Promotion.

2. A coffee shop offers a tenth drink free when nine stamps have been collected from previous purchases.

    Which of the following best describes this type of sales promotion? [1]

    A. ☐ Buy one, get one free (BOGOF).

    B. ☐ Loyalty scheme.

    C. ☐ Product trial.

    D. ☐ Sponsorship.

3. Which **one** of the following is a characteristic of the growth stage of the product life cycle? [1]

    A. ☐ Heavy promotion to encourage early sales.

    B. ☐ High research and development costs.

    C. ☐ Significant increase in sales.

    D. ☐ Slow decline in sales.

4. Celebrity endorsement and product placement are examples of: [1]

    A. ☐ Point of sale advertising.

    B. ☐ Psychological pricing.

    C. ☐ Public relations strategies.

    D. ☐ Sponsorship.

5. Which **one** of the following is considered an example of a non-digital advertising medium? [1]

    A. ☐ Blog.

    B. ☐ Cinema.

    C. ☐ Podcast.

    D. ☐ Website.

6. The sales for Watsons Tools are given in **Figure 1**.

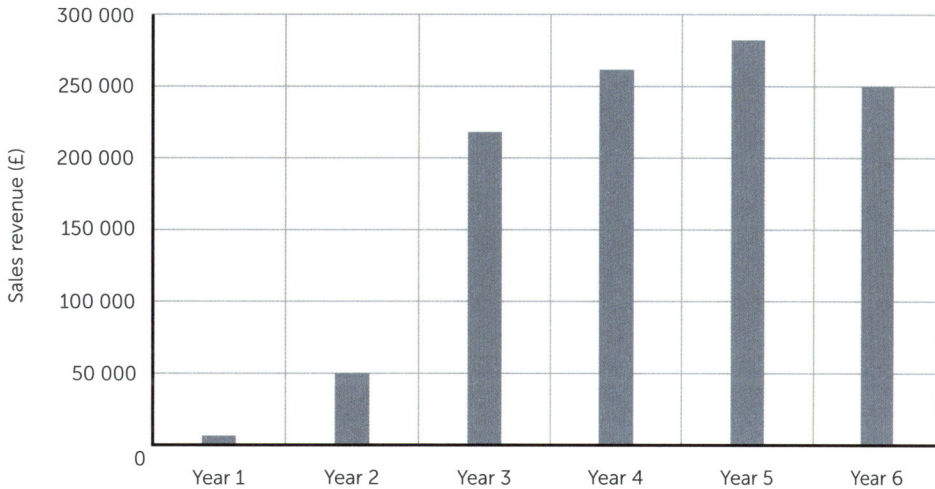

Figure 1

(a) Identify the most likely stage of the product life cycle in Year 5. [1]

(b) Describe **one** strategy the business could use to boost sales in Year 6. [3]

7. Your business needs to decide on a pricing strategy.

Draw a line to link **each** pricing strategy with the correct action.

You should draw **four** lines in total. [4]

	Set prices high initially, then lower them over time.
	Price products according to their actual value.
Competitive pricing	Add a percentage onto the costs of making the product.
Psychological pricing	Dynamically change prices depending on when, where and who is buying them.
Price skimming	Set prices based on those of other similar businesses.
Price penetration	Set a low initial price to maximise market share.
	Set prices to appear lower e.g. £99.95.

8. Jasmine and Gary own a high street retro game shop. They sell both video games and board games. They have noticed that fewer people are visiting the store area, and this is affecting their revenue. They are considering investing in an ecommerce website to accompany store sales.

(a) Explain **one** advantage to Jasmine and Gary of having a virtual store as well as a physical store. [2]

(b) The owners have noticed that similar games shops nearby are still busy and think this may be related to price.
Explain **one** reason why a business may need to know what price competitors are charging. [2]

(c) State **two** disadvantages of online retail to a business. [2]

9. You have taken ownership of a popular mobile car detailing business. You need to attract new customers in order to maintain growth. You are considering a promotional campaign to raise awareness of a new alloy wheel repair service.

Discuss whether you should use social media or radio to advertise the new service.

Your recommendation should include:

- An advantage and a disadvantage of social media
- An advantage and a disadvantage of radio
- A justification for your decision. [8]

5.1

APPROPRIATE FORMS OF OWNERSHIP FOR BUSINESS START-UPS

When an entrepreneur decides to start up a business, they have a number of different options for its formation. Each option will have an impact on the legal status of the business.

Limited and unlimited liability

If a business owner (entrepreneur) has **unlimited liability**, then they and the business are seen as the same legal entity. This is known as an **unincorporated** business. Any debts that the business has, will be the total responsibility of the owner. If the business cannot pay the debts off, then the owner may have to sell personal possessions to clear them. If an entrepreneur has **limited liability**, then they are seen as separate from the business in the eyes of the law. This is called **incorporation**, where the debts of the business are not regarded as personal debts of the owner. The entrepreneur is only liable for the amount of money that they have personally invested.

Types of ownership

Sole trader — Unlimited liability

💰 A **single owner** keeps or reinvests all the profits as they wish.

Advantages
- Quick and easy to set up.
- Sole trader makes all the decisions.
- Business' financial information is kept private.

Disadvantages
- Sole trader faces unlimited liability.
- No partners to share the decision making with which can be lonely and stressful.
- May be more difficult to raise finance.
- Business may not run if sole trader is off sick or takes holiday.

Partnership   **Unlimited liability**

Limited Liability Partnership (LLP)   **Limited liability**

A **partnership** is an unincorporated business which has two or more owners who share the risk. An **LLP** provides protection to each partner from personal liability beyond what they have already personally invested into the business.

💰 Profits are reinvested or shared amongst partners according to agreed ratios.

Advantages

- Each partner could contribute finances, bring ideas and different skills.
- The workload and responsibility for decisions can be shared between partners.
- Business' financial information is kept private.

Disadvantages

- Partners of standard partnerships face unlimited liability.
- There may be disagreements over decision making between the partners.
- An LLP requires a slightly more formal legal set up than a partnership.

Private limited company (ltd)   **Limited liability**

A private limited company is an incorporated business which is owned by **private shareholders**. Shares can only be sold privately, usually to friends and family.

💰 Profits are paid via dividends to shareholders. Directors appointed by the shareholders have full responsibility for decision making and the operation of the business.

Advantages

- Easier to raise finance by selling shares.
- Owners have limited liability.

Disadvantages

- Overall control could be lost.
- The company's accounts and financial information is not private.
- More legal paperwork involved when setting up as it is more complex.

Scott is looking to extend his hobby for fixing garden machinery to accept paid work. He works on his own in his garage. Scott has very few start-up costs and wants to make the transition into business as simple as possible

Discuss which form of ownership would be most suitable for Scott.   [3]

Scott has no other partners involved in the business, so a sole trader or limited company are the best options.[1] Of these, a limited company would require registration and additional paperwork to get started which Scott is hoping to avoid.[1] Whilst a limited company would protect Scott from being liable for the business' costs, it appears that he won't have many so a sole trader might be most suitable.[1] A sole trader is also quickest and simplest to set up.[1]

FRANCHISING

An entrepreneur has the option to set up as an independent business or set up as a **franchise**. A **franchisee** is licensed to sell the products or services of an already established business, known as the **franchisor**.

Franchise

The license given by the franchisor allows the new owner to trade using the name, products and equipment of the franchisor, whilst remaining independent. However, the franchisor will charge a **fee** in return, as well as taking a share of the business' revenues, known as a **royalty**.

Discuss the drawbacks to an owner of setting up a business as a franchisee. [6]

One drawback is that a franchisee cannot choose where to get supplies from.[1] This lack of control means that they have no room to shop around to find a cheaper supplier,[1] meaning that they are unable to reduce their variable cost by finding someone selling supplies for less.[1] Therefore, they may be unable to change the price that the product is sold for,[1] which could make them uncompetitive against other local independent competitors.[1] This could have a negative impact on sales levels,[1] causing the business not to sell enough products to break even.[1]

Other drawbacks include expensive start-up fees, royalty fees to the franchisor regardless of profits made, the impact of other franchisees affecting your own reputation, and other restrictions placed on the franchisee such as choice of location.

Why start as a franchise?

By setting up as a franchise rather than an independent business, the new owner is hoping to reduce the risks faced when starting a business. Risk is reduced because of the following reasons:

- **Brand name** is already established: This will mean that customers will recognise the business name and its products, so may be more likely to purchase products. The business will already have an established customer base.

- Access to **established products and processes**: Not only will the franchisee be able to sell products that customers already know about, they will also gain access to the franchisor's processes and equipment.

- Franchisor provides **training**: The franchisor will provide ongoing support for the franchisee. This is because it is in their interest that the business is successful too.

- Franchisor undertakes **advertising and promotion**: This means that there is one less thing for franchisee to do. The franchisor can afford to undertake expensive advertising that the individual owner may not be able to pay for if they were completely independent.

The responsibility for decision making in a franchise will belong with the owners and the franchisors jointly.

SOURCES OF CAPITAL FOR BUSINESS START-UPS AND EXPANSION

All businesses need sources of finance to set up the enterprise and for growth.

Internal sources of funding includes retained earnings (profits) and investment from within the enterprise, such as a sole trader's own savings. **External sources** of finance include banks, institutions, individuals and companies outside of the enterprise.

Using your own savings

Advantages

- No interest to pay on your own savings.
- Borrowing from family. Usually no or low interest payable.
- No debt created.
- No application forms to complete.
- Funds are immediately available.

Friends and family may offer financial support as a gift or a loan.

Disadvantages

- If the enterprise fails, the owner loses the money.
- Limited by what savings are available.
- Borrowing from family. May insist the money is paid back at any point or want to be consulted on how the money is spent which could harm the business.

66.762

External sources of finance

Loans

(Usually from a bank or building society.)

Advantages
- The interest rate is usually fixed for the entire loan period.
- Easy to budget for if it is a fixed repayment every month.
- Loan interest is generally lower than other sources of finance.
- Can borrow large sums.
- Lender gets no business shares.

Disadvantages
- Interest rates, fees or bank charges may apply.
- Failure to repay the loan may lead to bankruptcy and repossession of assets.
- Bank may want security (e.g. a fixed asset) to loan against.
- Time consuming application forms are required.

Business angel investment

Advantages
- Can also provide a source of advice and support.
- Do not have to pay interest or repayments.

Disadvantages
- May involve allowing them to make management decisions and/or giving them a share of the enterprise.

Crowdfunding

Advantages
- Quick way to raise finance with no fees.
- Alternative source if businesses struggle to get bank loans / are higher risk.
- Can test the reaction of the market to new ideas.
- Large sums can be raised.
- No security is required.

Disadvantages
- If you don't reach the funding target, money is returned to the investors.
- If you don't own copyright or a patent someone can steal your idea.
- Need to invest time and money to launch the project.

Grants

Advantages
- Grants do not always need paying back.
- Often free of interest and fees.

Disadvantages
- Only certain types of businesses are eligible.
- May be conditions attached to them which have to be fulfilled.
- Hard to get if limited funds are available for many businesses.

SUPPORT FOR ENTERPRISE

Many organisations and services are set up for businesses to use where they need support. They may provide specialist services or more general advice where entrepreneurs need it most.

	Advantages	Limitations
Finance providers, e.g. bank, business angel	• Provide finance for start-ups or expansion. • Can provide good advice to accompany the finance.	• Need to repay interest or part with a share in the business.
Local council enterprise department	• Likely to understand the local economy you operate in. • Can offer free advice to support SME growth.	• May not understand your own niche business. • May not be immediately available for advice or may provide a report weeks later.
Accountants	• Qualified, impartial advice. • Up to date advice. • Can save businesses far more than the fees they charge.	• Expensive. • Their financial advice may not be right for your business.
Solicitors	• Qualified professionals with trustworthy, confidential advice. • Up to date advice. • Unbiased advice.	• Expensive. • Need a solicitor experienced in a specific legal area. • A good solicitor may not be immediately available.
Friends and family	• Usually free • Usually available immediately	• Heavily biased. • May be unqualified to advise.
Chamber of Commerce (A network of business support organisations)	• Offer specialised support to growing businesses. • Can be a useful place to meet other entrepreneurs and share problems.	• Membership fees are required. • Regular meetings may not always be convenient or useful.
Government	• Valuable financial, emotional and technical support for first-time entrepreneurs. • Mentors and training available from some government divisions.	• Information overload means it isn't always clear what the right path is.
Charities	• Financial support and training offered. • Information and impartial advice.	• Limited in what they can provide owing to funding. • Often specific on who they will/can support.

EXAMINATION PRACTICE

1. Amy makes and sells jewellery by herself. She wants to invest in new machinery through the use of a loan.

    Which **one** of the following ownerships structures should Amy use to avoid personal liability for the investment loan should the company not succeed? [1]
    - A. ☐ Limited liability partnership.
    - B. ☐ Partnership.
    - C. ☐ Private limited company.
    - D. ☐ Sole trader.

2. Which **one** of the following is an advantage of running a business as a sole trader? [1]
    - A. ☐ Can keep all of the profits.
    - B. ☐ Company accounts are publicly available.
    - C. ☐ Easier to raise finance.
    - D. ☐ Unlimited liability.

3. Which **one** of the following is an advantage of accepting investment funds from a helpful friend? [1]
    - A. ☐ Formal application forms are not necessary.
    - B. ☐ Friend may insist in being consulted on how the funds are spent.
    - C. ☐ Friend may need the money back sooner than expected.
    - D. ☐ The investment may be lost which may damage the friendship.

4. Explain what is meant by 'unlimited liability'. [2]

5. Polly is considering opening an optician either as a franchise or as a sole trader.

    Analyse **two** advantages of franchise ownership compared with a sole trader. [6]

6. You are the sole shareholder of a limited business that has been offered investment for a new project by an angel investor and has an agreement in principle on a bank loan.

    (a) Discuss which of the options would be best for the business and provide a recommendation.

    Your recommendation should include:
    - An advantage and a disadvantage of angel investment
    - An advantage and a disadvantage of a bank loan
    - A justification for your decision. [8]

    (b) Suggest **two** alternative sources of investment that do not usually involve interest or fees. [2]

7. You need advice from an accountant about new laws surrounding taxation and profits within your industry.

    Explain **one** benefit and **one** limitation of seeking advice from an accountant. [4]

Section B contains 9 questions. All Section B questions will relate to a single scenario. The scenario will always be introduced at the start of Section B, and will develop through the section. Questions will consist of short, medium and longer points-based questions and one extended answer response marked by levels of response. Your answers should relate to the context of the scenario.

Katie owns a small café and has invited you to join her as a partner. The café is based in the centre of a busy town near shops and offices.

1. Give **two** reasons why Katie would want a partner in her business. [2]

2. Katie has asked you about a potential lunchtime desk delivery service the café could offer to local offices. You decide to conduct some market research by asking potential customers who visit the café.

   (a) State whether this is primary or secondary research. [1]

   (b) Explain the purpose of conducting market research in this way. [2]

   You are considering building a website to collect online orders for delivery if the service is popular.

   (c) Explain **one** disadvantage of taking orders for deliveries via an online sales channel. [2]

3. Katie has suggested that delivering to office workers may open up a new target market.
   Describe the segment that includes office workers. [3]

4. Analyse how the marketing mix may need to change for office deliveries. [3]

5. Market research has been positive and you are required to plan the costs of running a delivery service.
   A small business expansion grant is available from the local council.

   (a) Give **one** advantage and one disadvantage of getting a grant. [2]

   (b) Suggest **one** source of support and information on how best to set up a local delivery service. [1]

6. You are considering how best to promote the new delivery service to new and existing customers. Discuss whether you should use point of sale advertising or a competition to promote your new service. Your recommendation should include:

   - A benefit and limitation of using point of sale advertising
   - A benefit and limitation of using a competition
   - A justification for your decision.   [8]

Example answers

1.   A **partner** allows Katie to take more time off[1], to share the responsibilities and decision making[1], to split future **investment**[1] into the business and to bring additional **characteristics** and strengths into the business[1]. It is also less lonely for Katie.[1]

2.   (a) **Primary** research.[1]

      (b) To reduce **risk** / better understand **customer needs**[1] so that the service is more likely to be a success / make a **profit**.[1]

      (c) Digital sales involve **website development** and ongoing maintenance costs[1] which would make the service harder to **break-even**.[1] / Online selling may weaken the **customer relationship**[1] that has been built up through customers visiting the café in person.[1]

3.   Likely to be between 18 and 65.[1] Based locally to the café for faster deliveries.[1] **Income levels** will likely to be moderate as they are professionals/administrators rather than manual labourers.[1]

4.   The **product** is likely to need additional packaging[1] so that it can be transported safely and eaten tidily at a desk.[1] The **price** may need to increase to allow for the **costs** of delivery.[1] The **place** will change as they no longer need to visit the café to collect and purchase food.[1] **Promotion** of the café and the new service will need to widen as new customers will not know about the service.[1] **Advertising** for the service can be placed in the café[1] but further **promotions** using **leaflets** could be considered.[1]

5.   (a) There is usually no **interest** to pay on a **grant**[1] and the original amount is unlikely to need to be **repaid** either.[1] However, the business may not qualify for the grant[1] and could find that the available funds have run out or may not be available before they are needed to cover the start-up costs of the service.[1]

      (b) The **local council enterprise department** may have information and experience of this.[1] / Joining a local **chamber of commerce** will provide access to a group of other **entrepreneurs** who may have done the same thing for their own businesses.[1]

6.   **Point of sale advertising** would grab the attention of existing customer in the café as they pay for their **goods** but the advertising would only be effective with **existing customers**. *[Level 1 so far]*

      A **competition** could help launch the service by offering a free lunch for a month for example but an additional **campaign** to raise **awareness** of the competition would be required, which may add to the cost of the prize. *[Level 2 so far]*

      Overall, I would recommend the **point of sale advertising** as it would be relatively inexpensive to create and staff can explain it to customers as they come in with the hope that word of mouth would spread to customer colleagues. *[Level 3]*

      *(This question should be marked in accordance with the levels based mark scheme on page 59. Key terminology has been **emboldened** to illustrate how it has been used in sample responses.)*

EXAMINATION PRACTICE ANSWERS

Topic Area 1

1.   B – Confidence.   [1]

2.   D – Improved personal relationships.   [1]

3.   Personal relationships with family/friends/spouse,[1] financial wellbeing,[1] personal well-being/health,[1]
     work-life balance.[1]   [3]

4.   An entrepreneur will need to negotiate the best deals for raw materials and stock with their suppliers.[1] They will need to
     be able to negotiate to recruit good potential employees to ensure that both parties feel happy with any agreement.[1]
     Negotiation with resellers/banks/legal contracts to ensure the best outcomes.[1] Negotiate the sale of the business.[1]   [2]

5.   (a) To help others/to make a difference.[1] Self-satisfaction of helping/being a respected figure in the community.[1]
          Do not allow independence/financial return as he may already have that through other businesses.   [1]
     (b) David already runs businesses/may already be busy[1] so another business may require even more of his spare time
          and attention.[1] A new business is likely to require a lot of hours to set up[1] which will come at the cost of his social
          life or time spent on other enterprises.[1]   [2]
     (c) David may have to pay for his website upfront even though he may not have had a single sale.[1] This means that he
          may make a financial loss.[1]   [2]

Topic Area 2

1.   B – Find out what customers want.   [1]

2.   B – Qualitative data   [1]

3.   A – Generic information which may not apply to your business.   [1]

4.   (a) (i)   It is usually cheaper than primary research.[1] It can be less time consuming because information is more
                easily found.   [1]
          (ii) The information may be out of date.[1] The information gathered may not be specific or relevant to the business.[1]   [1]
     (b) If the business has unreliable data, then they may offer a service that isn't wanted[1]. This could be because they have
          not surveyed a representative sample of their target market[1]. This could mean a lot of money is wasted in designing
          the wrong pet grooming service[1], causing the business to have cash flow problems[1].   [3]
     (c) Social media could be used[1] so that customers could post reviews.[1] Surveys could be delivered in person or
          by email[1] which could gather responses to specific questions.[1] Contact forms could be made available on a
          website[1] for customers to email their thoughts.[1]   [2]

5.   Marketing is more efficient / less expensive,[1] because the market is divided up into smaller segments to focus on / which
     makes limited budgets go further.[1] The best way to reach customers is clearer,[1] because each segment will be based on /
     have similar customer characteristics.[1] Sales may increase,[1] because customers feel that their needs are more closely met
     / are more likely to become loyal / make repeat purchases.[1] Overall market share may increase,[1] because sales increase
     within each of several smaller segments / which decreases the risk of failure.[1]   [2]

1. A – Advertising. [1]

2. D – A cost that varies with the level of output. [1]

3. C – Loss. [1]

4. Fixed costs = £12,500
    Variable costs = £2.00 × 5,000 = £10,000
    Total costs = Fixed costs + variable costs = £12,500 + £10,000 = £22,500. [2]

5. A business will need cash to pay its employees/suppliers.[1] Without paying them, they would very quickly stop working for / supplying the business. As a result, the business would not be able to produce goods or provide a service.[1] [2]

6. (a) Fixed costs. [1]

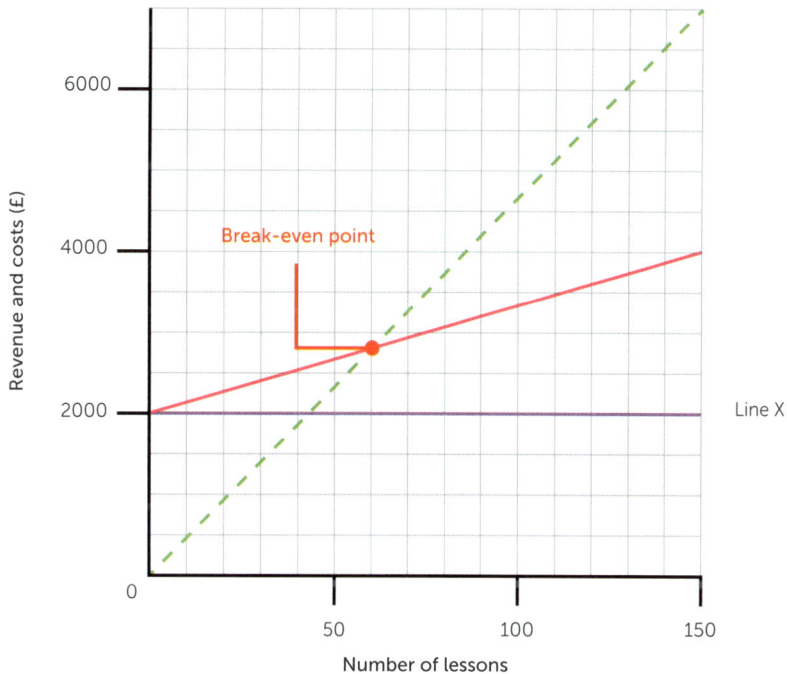

Break-even point

Line X

Revenue and costs (£)

Number of lessons

   (b) (i)   As given in green. [1]
       (ii) As shown above. [1]
   (c) Break-even = 2000 / (40 − 15)
                    = 2000 / 25
                    = 80 lessons
                                                                            [2]

   (d) 125 = 2000 / (selling price − 15)
       Selling price − 15 = 2000 / 125
       Selling price − 15 = 16
       Selling price = 16 + 15
       Selling price to break even = £31 [2]

7. Using cheaper raw materials in production of the product[1] will mean that variable costs per unit are lower[1]. This increases the difference between the selling price and the cost of making the product[1]. This will lower the amount needed to be sold to break even.
    A business can reduce its break even by increasing the selling price[1]. Therefore, the difference between price and variable costs will be greater[1], meaning they need to sell fewer products or services to cover the fixed costs[1]. [3]

1. C – Profit. [1]

2. B – Loyalty scheme. [1]

3. C – Significant increase in sales. [1]

4. C – Public relations strategies. [1]

5. B – Cinema. [1]

6. (a) Maturity. [1]

   (b) The business can start a new advertising campaign[1] to increase sales through raised awareness[1] or to attract new customers.[1]

   They could decrease the price of the product[1] since the development costs are likely to have been recovered[1] which may encourage more sales from those who previously could not afford the tools or from a new target market on lower incomes.[1]

   A new target market[1] could be sought to sell the tools in which would create a new set of potential customers.[1] This would increase sales again in that region and help to balance a decline of sales at times in multiple regions.[1]

   New packaging[1] could enhance the appeal of an old product[1] to increase sales with a new audience. The packaging could also be cheaper to produce[1] meaning that the company could lower costs as well.[1] [3]

7. [4]

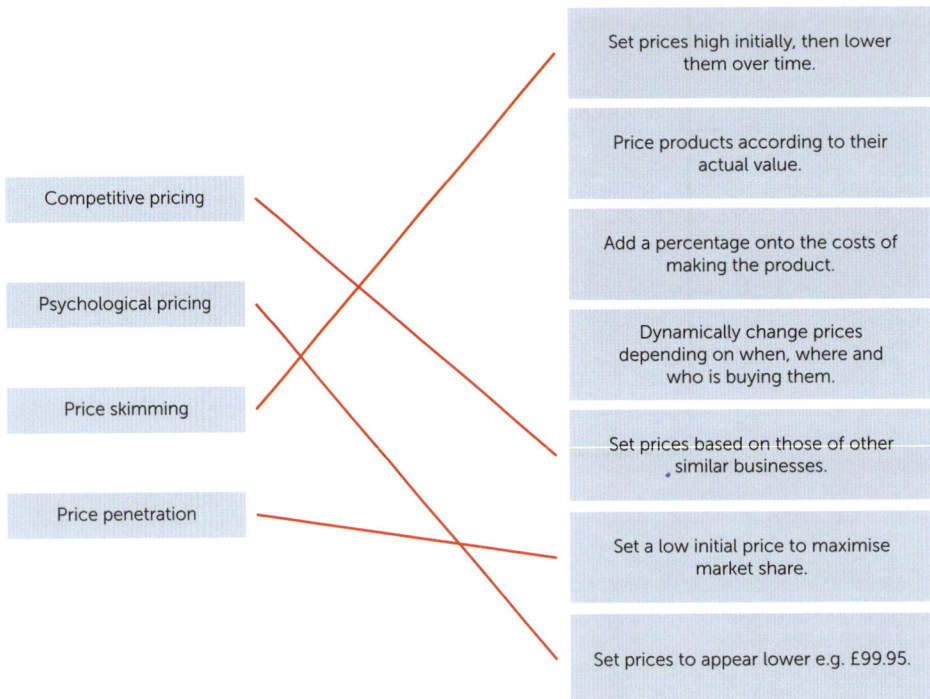

8. (a) They will be able to reach more of their target market[1] which may increase sales for Jasmine and Gary.[1] People who do not go to / live near the store can access[1] and buy products / can make purchases.[1] An ecommerce site may increase brand awareness and exposure for the game shop[1] which may attract more customers.[1] A virtual store can be open 24/7[1] which may increase sales after the high street shop has closed.[1] [2]

   (b) It is important because a business may have a similar product to its rivals[1]. If they charged a much higher price, they may not receive many sales which could lead to the business not selling enough products to breakeven[1]. [2]

   (c) Initial and ongoing website development and maintenance costs can be high.[1] Potentially high infrastructure costs of warehousing, distribution and dealing with returns.[1] Security and fraud associated with online transaction systems can cost a business heavily[1] if they are not protected against it using the latest security systems. Advertising costs can be high with an online only store as there is no high street store front to generate awareness.[1] It is difficult to build trust with customers online without a human face-to-face connection.[1] [2]

9. This type of question will be marked using a Levels Based Marks Scheme. See **page 59** for details.

Indicative content:

Social media

Advantages:
- Wide reach
- Can target specific groups, e.g. people of driving age.
- Can use animations and video to draw attention to the adverts.
- Can easily be updated and amended according to response.

Disadvantages:
- Adverts may get lost amongst millions of other posts online.
- Needs constant updates and planning to create an ongoing campaign.
- People may respond negatively to the posts / post negative comments.

Radio

Advantages:
- Affordable.
- Wide reaching audience.
- Can use jingles and specific sounds to catch attention.
- Can time the adverts to appeal to listeners/drivers likely to be in their cars at certain times of day, e.g. rush hour.

Disadvantages:
- No visual appeal.
- Limited attention from listeners.
- More expensive than social media.

Justification

Accept either method as suitable depending on the justification. This may be based on the relative merits of each method and the value for money for the business.

Example response:

Social media can be used to include 'before and after' pictures of successful repairs so that customers can see the results. Radio could be used to create an ongoing campaign which becomes recognised and is useful to target drivers whilst they are passively listening. A social media campaign may however, require more time to plan and post ongoing adverts to maintain the campaign which would take more time from the business. A radio advert would take time to plan and record, but then it is done. However, the costs of creating a radio advert may be much higher.

I would recommend that radio be used to attract new customers as listeners would likely be car owners if the advert is played during peak traffic hours and would not require any more time invested after the advert has been produced. [8]

1. C – Private limited company. [1]

2. A – Can keep all of the profits. [1]

3. A – Formal application forms are not necessary. [1]

4. The business owner(s) have personal responsibility[1] to pay all of the debts of the business should it have to close.[1]
    This may mean selling personal assets to cover the costs.[1] [2]

5. **Indicative content:**
    The brand name is already established[1] so will attract sales from day one of trading[1] as customers will be familiar with the brand / have established trust in the brand.[1]
    The franchisor will be able to provide access to proven products and processes[1] which will make business more efficient.[1] This will save Polly time / from making mistakes experimenting with other options.[1]
    Training will be provided[1] to give the franchise the best chance of success,[1] so Polly will feel supported and less on her own.[1]
    Marketing and promotion will be managed centrally[1] which saves having to pay for this directly[1] and frees up the time for Polly to concentrate on other parts of the business.[1] [6]

6. (a) This type of question will be marked using a Levels Based Marks Scheme. See **page 59** for details.
        Indicative content:
        Angel investment often comes with advice and support, (✓) which I can use to help direct the business more effectively. (✓) This will help avoid common mistakes. (✓) There is no monthly repayment to be made (✓) which will help the cash flow of the business / not increase the outgoings. (✓) This will provide more cash to be spent on other projects that may help the business. (✓) Whilst there is no interest to pay on angel investment, I would have to give away a percentage share of the business. (✓)

        A loan would avoid needing to give up any share of the business (✓) but would incur and monthly interest repayment until the loan is repaid in full. I would need to make the repayments each month otherwise the bank may take possession of assets to the value of the original loan. (✓)

        Overall, I would recommend a business angel investor as they are likely to provide help and be motivated to support me in making the business a success as a shareholder. (✓) They would also help share some of the decision making which would be reassuring and less lonely. (✓) [8]

    (b) Two from: Family and friends,[1] crowdfunding[1] or grants[1]. [2]

7. An accountant is professionally qualified to give advice which can be trusted.[1] They will treat information about the business finances as confidential which would avoid business secrets being made public.[1] The advice will also be up to date which means the business will comply with the latest government changes.[1] Even though their fees may be expensive, they may make greater savings in the accounts and avoid any potential fines or costly investigations.[1]
    The advice is expensive so the business will need to have sufficient earnings available to cover their costs.[1]
    They may not understand the nature of the industry the business operates in so their advice may not be perfectly suitable / applicable for this business.[1] [4]

LEVELS BASED MARK SCHEME FOR EXTENDED RESPONSE QUESTIONS

Questions that require extended writing use mark bands. The whole answer will be marked together to determine which mark band it fits into and which mark should be awarded within the mark band. The levels of response each describe the top of the band.

Level	Mark band	Descriptor
Level 3	7–8 marks	A thorough discussion which: • shows clear analysis of advantages and disadvantages of both options • makes a justified decision, using appropriate context • consistently uses appropriate terminology • shows detailed understanding
Level 2	4–6 marks	An adequate discussion which: • shows sound analysis of an advantage and a disadvantage of both options • makes limited use of appropriate context • uses some appropriate terminology • shows sound understanding
Level 1	1–3 marks	A basic discussion which: • shows limited analysis of an advantage or a disadvantage of an option • makes limited use of appropriate context • makes limited or no use of appropriate terminology • shows limited understanding
Level 0	0 marks	Response is missing or not worthy of credit.

NOTES, DOODLES AND EXAM DATES

....
....
....
....
....
....
....
....
....
....
....
....
....
....
....

Doodles

INDEX

Symbols

4Ps 25, 27

A

accountants 50
adding value 37
advertising 16, 37
advertising medium 27
age 13
analysis 12
angel investment 49
auction sites 35

B

bank 50
billboards
blogs 28
books 10
break-even 20, 64
break-even point 21
bricks and clicks 34
bricks and mortar shops 34
business
   angel 50
   angel investment 49
   generated posts 29
buy one get one free (BOGOF)
      30

C

capital 48
cash 22
celebrity endorsement 32
census 11
chamber of commerce 50
change 3
characteristics 2, 13
charities 50
cinema 28
communication 2
competition 26
competitions 30, 53
competitive
   edge 14
   pricing 41
competitor data 10

components 16
confidence 2
consumer trials 9
costs 16
costs per unit 16
creativity 2
crowdfunding 49
customer
   needs 6, 13, 14
   retention 14, 27, 30

D

data 12
decision making 6
decline 36
determination 2
development 36
digital
   advertising 27, 28
   sales 34, 35
discounting 30, 37
disposable income 6, 39
downloads 35
Dyson, Sir James 2

E

e-commerce 35
endorsement 32
enterprise support 50
entrepreneur 2
extension strategies 37, 39

F

face-to-face selling 34
feedback 29
financial
   rewards 3
   risks 4
fixed costs 16, 21, 64
   per unit 64
focus groups 8
forms of ownership 45
formulae 64
four Ps 25
franchise 47
free gifts 31
friends and family 50

G

gap in the market 6
gender 13
goods 25, 37
government 50
   publications 11
grant 49, 52
growth 36

H

health 4
high street shop 34

I

income 13
income levels 39
independence 3
influencers 32
innovation 2
insolvency 22
insurance 16
internal data 10
internet 11
interviews 8
introduction 36

K

Keynote 11

L

leaflets 27
liability 45
lifestyle 13
limited liability 45
limited liability partnership 46
loan interest 16
loans 49
local council enterprise
      department 50
location 13
loss 19
loyalty 14
   schemes 31

M

magazines 28
marketing
  mix 25, 26, 39, 52
  targeted 14
marketplace sites 35
market
  research 52
      companies 11
      primary methods 8
      purpose of 6
      secondary 10
  segmentation 13, 14, 26
  trends 6
maturity 36
Mintel 11

N

negotiation 2
new markets 38
new packaging 38
newspapers 10, 27

O

observations 9
occupation 13
offers 30
online
  auction sites 35
  banner 28
  sales 34
ownership 45

P

packaging 16, 38
partnership 46
personal relationships 4
pilot 9
place 25, 34
podcasts 29
point of sale advertising 31, 53
pop-up 28
posters
potential market 6
press release 33
price 25, 39, 40
  changes 37
  penetration 40
  skimming 37, 40

primary market research 8
private limited company (ltd) 46
product 25, 26, 37
  development 6
  life cycle 26, 36, 39
  placement 32
  trials 31
production 16
  costs 39
profession 13
profit 16, 19, 22, 64
promotion 25
promotional mix 30
prototype 9
psychological pricing 41
public relations (PR) 32

Q

qualitative data 12
quantitative data 12
questionnaires 8

R

radio 27
raw materials 16
rearranging a formula 18
relationships 4
rent 16
retention 14, 27, 30
revenue 16, 18, 21
risk 2, 3, 4, 6

S

salaries 16
sales 18
sales promotion 30
savings 48
secondary market research 10
segment 13, 14, 26, 52
self-satisfaction 3
service 25
services 37
SMS texts 29
social media 29, 35
sole trader 45
solicitors 50
sources of capital 48
sponsorship 31
support 50, 52
surveys 8, 11

T

targeted marketing 14
technology 26
test marketing 9
third-party-generated posts 29
total cost per unit 64
total costs 17, 21, 64
total revenue 18, 64
total variable costs 16, 64
trade magazines 10
traditional advertising 27

U

unlimited liability 45
utilities 16

V

variable cost per unit 64
variable costs 16
video 29
vlogs 28

W

wages 16
website 28, 35
well-being 4
what-if analysis 20
Which? 11
work-life balance 4

FORMULAE

Total costs	= Fixed costs + Variable costs
Total cost per unit	= Fixed costs + Variable costs
Total variable costs	= Variable cost per unit × Number of units sold
Variable cost per unit	= Total variable costs ÷ Number of units sold
Fixed costs	= Total costs − Variable costs
Fixed costs per unit	= (Total costs − Variable costs) ÷ Number of units sold
Total revenue	= Selling price × Number of units sold
Profit	= Total revenue − Total costs
Break-even	= Fixed costs ÷ (Selling price − Variable cost per unit)

If your final answer to a calculation is correct, full marks will usually be given. However, some questions may specifically ask you to show your workings so that your thought process can be assessed. You can still gain marks in questions that require working to be shown, even if the final answer is incorrect. For this reason, it is good practice to show working in all calculation questions as it may still be possible for examiners to award you some marks.

EXAMINATION TIPS

With your examination practice, use a boundary approximation for the examined unit using the following table. Be aware that boundaries are usually a few percentage points either side of this.

Grade	Level 2				Level 1		
	Distinction*	Distinction	Merit	Pass	Distinction	Merit	Pass
Code	2*	D2	M2	P2	D1	M1	P1
Boundary	90%	80%	70%	60%	50%	40%	30%

1. Be prepared with a black pen, a calculator, and a ruler.

2. Read each question carefully as some students give answers to questions they think are appearing rather than the actual question.

3. Try to not repeat the question in the first line of your response. It will not score you any marks, but simply wastes your time. Avoid losing marks by not finishing the paper.

4. Try not to repeat the same points in your answers. Only the first will gain marks.

5. Focus your responses on the scenario or context in the question and consider the impact on the business or the concept in the question. Use the information you have been given in the question and make sure you reference it in your answer.

6. Learn and understand each of the different types of costs.

7. Learn each of the calculations required and practice rearranging equations.

8. In calculation questions, marks may be awarded for workings out if the final answer is incorrect. Make sure to show your working in case you make a mistake and the answer is incorrect. Workings also help you check through your own answers more quickly at the end of an exam.

9. Test yourself on pricing strategies and franchising as these topics are often poorly understood.

10. Become familiar with break-even charts and how they are constructed. You will not be expected to draw a break-even graph in the exam but you may be asked to interpret one or complete one that is already partially drawn.

11. When explaining your points, you need to use clear connectives to show that you are developing the point you have made and not moving onto a separate point. These connectives include; 'thus', 'therefore', 'this means that', 'this leads to', 'because' and 'as a consequence'. This demonstrates your skills of analysis which are assessed in medium and longer answer questions.

12. Avoid undeveloped answers such as 'quick', 'simple', 'fast' and 'easy'. These cannot be awarded marks.

13. Each question starts with a command word. Make sure you fully understand what each command word requires you to do. Reading the command verbs at the start of this guide will help you with this.

14. Answer questions in the spaces provided. If this is not possible, for instance, you have deleted a wrong answer, indicate the location of the corrected answer on the paper (e.g. 'see next page' or 'my answer is on the last blank page').

Good luck!

Revision, re-imagined

These guides are everything you need to ace your exams and beam with pride. Each topic is laid out in a beautifully illustrated format that is clear, approachable and as concise and simple as possible.

They have been expertly compiled and edited by subject specialists, highly experienced examiners, industry professionals and a good dollop of scientific research into what makes revision most effective. Past examination questions are essential to good preparation, improving understanding and confidence.

- Hundreds of marks worth of examination style questions
- Answers provided for all questions within the books
- Illustrated topics to improve memory and recall
- Specification references for every topic
- Examination tips and techniques
- Free Python solutions pack (CS Only)

Absolute clarity is the aim.

Explore the series and add to your collection at **www.clearrevise.com**

Available from all good book shops

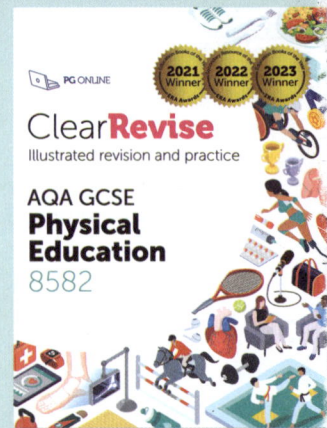

ClearRevise
Illustrated revision and practice
AQA GCSE **Physical Education** 8582

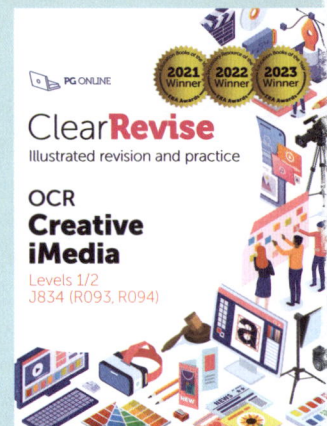

ClearRevise
Illustrated revision and practice
OCR **Creative iMedia**
Levels 1/2
J834 (R093, R094)

ClearRevise
Illustrated revision and practice
AQA GCSE **English Language** 8700

ClearRevise
Illustrated revision and practice
Edexcel GCSE **History 1HI0**
Weimar and Nazi Germany, 1918–39
Paper 3

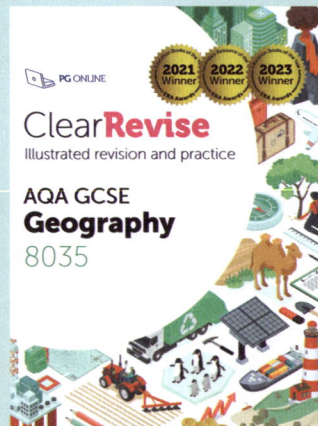

ClearRevise
Illustrated revision and practice
AQA GCSE **Geography** 8035

ClearRevise
Illustrated revision and practice
OCR GCSE **Computer Science** J277

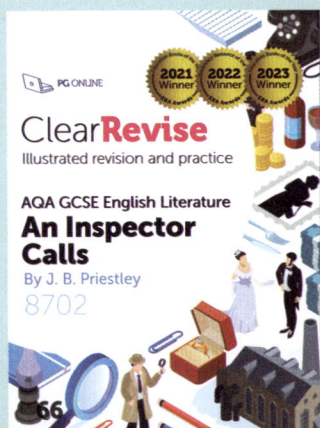

ClearRevise
Illustrated revision and practice
AQA GCSE English Literature **An Inspector Calls**
By J. B. Priestley
8702

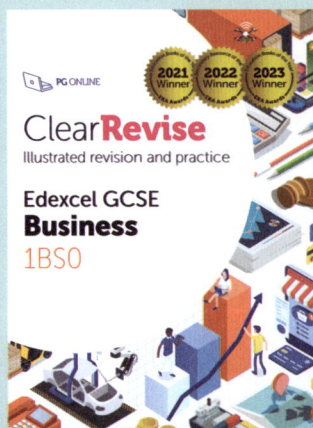

ClearRevise
Illustrated revision and practice
Edexcel GCSE **Business** 1BS0

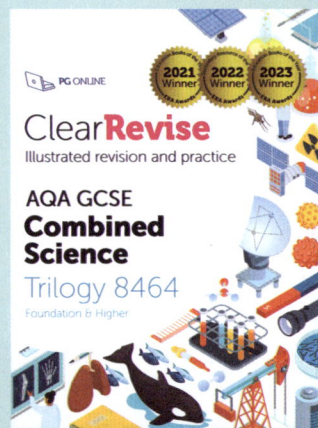

ClearRevise
Illustrated revision and practice
AQA GCSE **Combined Science**
Trilogy 8464
Foundation & Higher

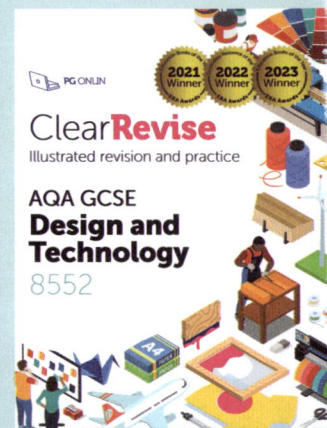

ClearRevise
Illustrated revision and practice
AQA GCSE **Design and Technology** 8552